Quench Not The Spirit

Quench Not The Spirit

Edward Harding

Life Changing Books

**Marshalls
New Wine Press**

Life Changing Books
Marshall Morgan & Scott
3 Beggarwood Lane, Basingstoke, Hants, RG23 7LP, UK

New Wine Press
PO Box 17, Chichester, W. Sussex, UK

First published by Marshall Morgan & Scott
and New Wine Press in 1984

British Library C.I.P.

Harding, Edward
  Quench not the spirit.
  1. Holy spirit
  I. Title
  231'.3   BT121.2

  ISBN 0 551 01155 6 Marshalls
  ISBN 0 947852 01 8 New Wine Press

Printed in Great Britain by
Hunt Barnard Printing Ltd., Aylesbury, Bucks.

Contents

Foreword

If you are a comfortable, complacent, luke-warm religious Christian and happy to remain so, then this book is not for you for it will challenge, rebuke and stir you up. For those who desire to mature in the Lord, however, and who wish to see Christ being formed in their lives this book will confirm much, challenge many areas which have been assumed as correct, and rebuke any lazy or compromising attitude which may have crept in unawares.

In his broad sweep Ed Harding courageously deals with areas of theological importance and controversy in these days of renewal, as well as giving practical, down-to-earth guidelines to enable us to 'walk in the Spirit'. 'As iron sharpeneth iron, so one man sharpens another' Proverbs 27:17, and the purpose of this book is that we might be finely honed.

Ed Harding has a well-reasoned yet uncomplicated faith and he is receiving increasing recognition for his direct, easily understood teaching. I welcome the challenge this book brings and heartily recommend it — it is good medicine for us all.

Roger Price
Bognor Regis
July 1984

Part I

How we quench the Spirit in our corporate life

Introduction

Some years ago, during the Carter administration at the White House, a new concept was introduced into government called 'zero budgeting'. It simply meant that instead of merely repeating what had been done the previous year, everything had to be justified afresh, in other words right back to square one – what was being done, why, and whether it should continue. The results of this approach were so eye-opening and so radical that opposition immediately arose to prevent it being implemented, despite a recognition that it was in fact correct! Nobody fully realised until then just how much of what was being done bore little relation to what was actually needed, and why so much had continued from year to year.

Writing this book has involved a similar approach, going right back to the basic biblical principles of the way God wants His church to be, which is why each chapter takes its title from a bible verse. Even allowing for cultural changes the first believers would scarcely recognise what is currently 'the Church', for we have generally ignored the biblical model which they experienced and different groups have introduced their own system and structure. Indeed the concept of the clergy with which we are so familiar was not introduced until Origen in the third century, so if we want to return to the early Church, as so many say they wish to, then the implications are considerable!

The wind of the Holy Spirit is blowing through the Church, and there are opportunities to change, if we will take them. God wants to prepare the Bride of Christ for Jesus and will work wherever He is allowed to. When new wine is added to old it causes increased fermentation and hyperactivity. This is currently happening in many places as God seeks to renew His people. It will inevitably cause a separation, as Paul indeed says it will (1 Corinthians 11:19). This will centre around the authority of the Bible, the priesthood of all believers, gifts and ministries of the Holy Spirit, and church leadership. All these are covered in the book because they are live issues in the process of renewal and will always appear when it takes place. Ultimately the separation will lead to a visible manifestation of the true Body of Christ on one hand, and the Apostate Church on the other. We are currently seeing the beginning of this with activity in both camps. God is bringing together the Body of Christ and preparing it to be the Bride of Jesus, while moves are afoot for the Apostate Church to merge together. It will not of course be known by that name, but the spirit of Antichrist, which means *other* Christ is going to present a different Jesus to the world, but it will not be of God, rather a counterfeit in preparation for the False Prophet. This is why we need to hear what the Spirit is saying to the Church now, because the prophetic scenario warns us what will happen and to beware, because the devil wants to deceive even the elect (Matthew 24:24).

All of us have our own cultural and spiritual

8

background that affects our thinking. It is therefore only fair that I disclose mine, as I do not want to seem to be prejudiced and have a limited view based on limited experience! I have been in the Church of England both as an unbeliever, or at least not born again, as well as a born-again believer. A number of years were spent in both charismatic and non-charismatic Anglican and Baptist churches before joining an independent fellowship, where I have been for the last seven years and in which I am now an elder. During these years I have been in some of the best known churches in the country and listened to the best known speakers. I have seen God work with many different people in a variety of contexts, and also seen at first hand organised resistance! The title of the book 'Quench not the Spirit' grew out of a need to appeal to believers to be aware of the eternal purposes of God for His Church in relation to history and prophecy, to be willing to introduce God's order for church government and meetings, and to be willing individually to submit our lives to the Word of God.

The book is divided into three parts. The first examines the way we restrict the Holy Spirit in our corporate life together. The second covers the main areas where we find it hard to allow God to have His perfect way in our individual lives, and the third section considers how to press on with God, how to lead a fruitful life and the marks of the early Church.

The aim of the book is to give you fresh insight into God's purposes and desires for His children. I hope that there will be much that you can use and apply in your own situation. The Holy Spirit is the Spirit of Truth as well as of power, and He desires truth in the inward parts and for us to apply the truth of biblical revelation to our lives.

My prayer is that this book will be used by the Lord to

speak to His people, build up His Church, and prepare His bride.

May God bless you and speak to you through it.

Edward Harding.
Chichester
May 1984

1

Give us a king

1 Samuel 8:6

Have you ever wondered why Israel never had a king but only judges up to the time of Saul? There were many men who could quite easily have called themselves kings and fulfilled that role – Abraham, Moses or Joshua to name but three. Instead God decided that His chosen people would have no king, because He Himself would be their king and go out at the head of His people to fight their battles. This has always been God's intention for His people and also that there should be prophets among them to bring the word of the Lord. This principle remains equally valid today.

At the time of Samuel Israel had been ruled by a series of judges including Gideon and Samson, who were acting as God's representatives in both teaching the people and bringing deliverance from their enemies. However by the end of the Book of Judges acceptance of the rule of God's law had deteriorated to such an extent that the last sentence reads: 'In those days Israel had no king; everyone did as he saw fit.' (Judges 21:25 NIV).

By the time of 1 Samuel the situation was still pretty bad with anarchy abounding. Eli's sons Hophni and Phinehas were installed as priests but they were completely away from the Lord, treating the sacrifices with contempt. In this situation God raised up Samuel as prophet and priest, and Israel returned to order. However Samuel's sons did not follow their father's example and as Samuel began to get old the people decided that they had had enough and they wanted a king. They were not willing to have God as king because the other nations seemed to be stronger and more successful with their human kings, so complained to Samuel. 'They said to him, "You are old, and your sons do not walk in your ways; now appoint a king to lead us, such as all the other nations have." But when they said, "Give us a king to lead us," this displeased Samuel; so he prayed to the Lord. And the Lord told him: "Listen to all that the people are saying to you; it is not you they have rejected as their king, but me. As they have done from the day I brought them up out of Egypt until this day, forsaking me and serving other gods, so they are doing to you. Now listen to them; but warn them solemnly and let them know what the king who will reign over them will do."' Samuel then warns them exactly what will happen, but still they insist. 'But the people refused to listen to Samuel. "No", they said. "We want a king over us. Then we shall be like all the other nations, with a king to lead us and to go out before us and fight our battles."' (1 Samuel 8:5–21 NIV).

The whole point was that God did not want them to be like the other nations. He had fought their battles for them when they were occupying the land, such as taking Jericho and Ai, yet still they demanded a king.

The purpose of this illustration is that we can culturally and temperamentally be exactly the same. We want strong visible leadership in the church and nation and are reluctant for God to be king directly, or for things to be run His way. There is a sense of security and stability if there is a visible king.

Genesis 14 illustrates this desire for the safety of kingship. Abram rescues Lot from the four kings that have attacked Sodom, and yet Lot still returns to that corrupt regime under king Bera and misses the opportunity to break free and join Abram. He felt safer under the newly victorious king despite his 'success' being totally due to Abram's 318 trained men, and returned to Sodom's apparent security, with the result that he had to be rescued again later. Meanwhile Abram, who was walking by faith and knew he was a foreigner and stranger in the land, meets Melchizedeck king of Salem, priest of God Most High, who blesses him and Abram gives him a tenth of everything. The contrast is between the apparent safety of organised leadership with a king and city walls on one hand and the walk of faith living in tents with Abraham and God as king on the other.

The situation in the church today is similar, in that we can choose an authoritarian structured leadership that runs the church like a king, whereas God wants to be both our king and our security and has enabled us to have direct access to Him as kings and priests in our own right. One of the most significant revelations to the Church today, on which the whole question of church structure and organisation hinges, is the *priesthood of all believers* stated in Revelation 1:6 'Unto him that loved us, and washed us from our sins in his own blood, and hath made us *kings and priests* unto God and his Father; to him be glory and dominion for ever and ever. Amen' (Revelation 1:5–6 AV).

Jesus has made *us* kings and priests to serve God the Father. The biblical significance of this statement is that there is no longer any distinction between priest and people, clergy and laity as far as God is concerned. In the Church the number of priests is the same as the number of believers, but we have artificially reclassified them into two groups with different titles and functions. God never intended for one man to be 'the priest' and carry the weight of any church, nor to have the gifts necessary to be the omnicompetent multiministry man at the front. If you are an ordinary member of a church you need to see that your minister is actually meant to be one minister among many, and not the preacher/pastor taking the service each week.

Culture and tradition have been allowed to influence us more than the Bible, with the result that church services often bear no relation to the biblical model of participation and shared ministry, and are in essence led by the minister acting as a priest on behalf of the people. Even the physical design of churches right from Saxon and Norman times is based on this premise, with the transept acting as a barrier between the clergy, choir and congregation. The altar is a long way from the ordinary believer, and in those days the light was so poor that a sort of mystique was created about what happened up at the altar. This resembles the Old Testament idea of only the priest being allowed into the Holy of Holies as a representative of the people.

The significance of the curtain of the temple being torn in two must not be undervalued, because it was a direct and visible sign not just that Man was reconciled to God but that *direct access* was being given for the first time to the very throne of God, and God was abolishing the old priesthood. Jesus Himself was the Great High Priest and has made *us* a royal priesthood (1 Peter 2:9). The Levitical priesthood was inadequate (Hebrews 7:11) and merely a pointer to the one who was to come as the Great High Priest. Hebrews 9 and 10 cover this whole area and of course were written to the Jews precisely because it was a problem for them to accept this. It is equally important to us to be in the New Covenant and not reliving the Old in our type of worship.

'For Christ did not enter a manmade sanctuary that was only a copy of the true one; he entered heaven itself, now to appear for us in God's presence. Nor did he enter heaven to offer himself again and again, the way the high priest enters the Most Holy Place every year with blood that is not his own. Then Christ would have had to suffer many times since the creation of the world. But now he has appeared once for all at the end of the ages to do away with sin by the sacrifice of himself.' (Hebrews 9:24–26 NIV).

This wonderful truth now gives us direct access to God. It is important to see that the Levitical priesthood has been abolished, because if you still believe that it is valid and necessary it not only denies the completed work of Christ, but also denies Christians the revelation of the freedom they have come into, where they can confess their sins direct to God and be forgiven. All believers are now priests in their own right and represent themselves.

It is important to establish this foundational truth in relation to church structure because it affects the way we see both ourselves and the leadership of the church we are in. No longer do we need any mediator or intermediary to represent us before God as we are now all part of the Body of Christ, that mystery not fully revealed until after the Resurrection and the Day of Pentecost. We now have to look at the biblical model as God's ideal, see how the Church has moved away from that, and how to get back to it in these days of renewal. First of all the Head of the Church is the Lord Jesus Christ and all believers are automatically part of the Body of Christ. The head is in heaven with the body here on the earth, and one day soon we shall be united together. As in the human body the head sends messages *direct* to each part of the body. For example, to move my hand the message doesn't go to the neck which then tells the arm to move the hand. It goes direct, and so it is with the Lord. An example of this is specific prayer. God, who knows everything, hears the prayer of a believer saying he needs a change of car. He prays direct to the head and doesn't have to make the need public. Christ, the head, tells another Christian to provide either partially or in total, so that the need and the provision are linked up, and the body blessed. Possibly the word of knowledge may be used, where God tells a Christian of another's need, and that person responds having received what the need is, supernaturally from the head. This is true body ministry, and we should expect it to be the norm and not the exception. Unfortunately those who claim to have heard from the Lord are viewed with suspicion and either considered arrogant, superspiritual or odd in many churches, whereas we should *all* hear regularly from God. His sheep hear His voice, if they listen for it. The principle of direct access to the head means that revelation is not passed down through a hierarchy of leadership, where someone has to ask God on your behalf. Churches need to be modelled with this in mind recognising both plurality of leadership and corporate participation as part of the way God planned for the Body of Christ to function. Despite Roman Catholic claims, there is neither historical nor biblical evidence for Peter either being the first pope or for apostolic succession. Other books cover this more fully, but Peter describes himself as one of the *elders* (plural) and part of a team with plurality of leadership (1 Peter 5:1).

Although the Body of Christ as the worldwide Church is one, God never intended it to be run like a multinational corporation with a president, vice-president and executives. The very reverse is closer to the truth, with *many* leaders emerging from a group of believers and being appointed as elders within autonomous self-governing churches. The idea of taking the strongest people out of a church, training them elsewhere for three years, and then sending them somewhere totally different to run another church is quite alien to the biblical pattern, even if God still uses individuals who go that route. The early churches had a group of elders (presbuteros), never one man running a church single-handed, with deacons acting in their role of administrators. There were of course the original apostles and many believers were sent out as church planters, particularly at the time of the Jewish Diaspora in the early years, and had an apostolic ministry in relation to that church, but wherever a church was planted elders were appointed (Titus 1:5) and that church was self-governing, even if visited by the apostles.

Parallel to the new Christian 'churches of The Way', as they were called, were the synagogues on the old priestly model. The pagan religions were also structured this way. It was a hard readjustment for the traditional Jewish believers, many of whom wanted to maintain the old traditions, to see that God had actually changed the whole basis of their relationship to Him and therefore the way a meeting or service should be structured and run.

In these days of renewal God is wanting to bring us back to these fundamental principles, however radical and challenging they may be, and seek to re-establish plurality of leadership under God as king and corporate participation through the various gifts and ministries. The recent emergence of so many flourishing fellowships would not have happened if the 'mainline' churches had applied these principles and broken out of the traditional mould. Some groups are able to respond more easily than others and to move towards this goal. We must be aware what the Holy Spirit is saying to the Church, and be prepared to adjust our ways to conform to His.

The starting point towards this has to be autonomy and local freedom, even if a church or fellowship is associated with others of the same denomination or grouping. Unless the local Body of Christ is directly relating to the Head, and therefore hearing direct and moving ahead in the way they believe God is leading their eldership, there is a risk of missing all that the Lord has for them and for a programme to be imposed from outside based on someone else's expectation of how they should function and develop. Any form of outside control tends to restrict the freedom to move ahead purely looking unto Jesus as the head, who is actually able to speak to the believers directly Himself. Of course this does not invalidate input from outside, but it should be in the form of encouragement, help and support for the developing ministries within a local group, not the exercise of rulership over the believers in an authoritarian structure where they are automatically expected to submit meekly or be considered rebellious!

Within this independent group of believers there will be many gifts and ministries at varying stages of growth, some seeds, some plants, and they need the right climate to grow and be fruitful. One of the best ways of achieving this is to have housegroups of a dozen or so people with one or preferably two leaders as this will achieve two main goals. Firstly it involves all the members of a church or fellowship, and gets them to look at their own role and involvement in the life and growth of the group, including seeking to meet each others needs both spiritually and practically. Secondly it shares the weight of responsibility placing it at the point where needs can best be known and met, thus freeing the leadership to be more directly concerned with seeking God for directional guidance and receiving the Word of the Lord for the church or fellowship. In essence it's meant to be a team ministry with *everyone* in the team and each finding their role and ministry.

'We have different gifts, according to the grace given us. If a man's gift is prophesying, let him use it in proportion to his faith. If it is serving, let him serve; if it is teaching, let him teach; if it is encouraging, let him encourage; if it is contributing to the needs of others, let him give generously; if it is leadership, let him govern diligently; if it is showing mercy, let him do it cheerfully.' (Romans 12:6–8 NIV).

In this passage the one who prophesies, and even the one who teaches, is not necessarily the one who leads. Team ministry is meant to avoid the elevation of one-man ministries. Far too many churches are known by their ministers, and we should not be seeking a name for ourselves in God's Church or even be pushing our own individual ministry. Faithfulness to what we have is the goal and it is up to the Lord how He chooses to use us and what doors *He* opens.

Part of the recognition of the priesthood of all believers implies that there should be no distinction as far as dress is concerned. The wearing of clerical clothes, particularly the dog collar, perpetuates the artificial distinction and creates expectations on both sides. There are occasionally times where it may be appropriate as identification, such as hospital visiting, but in general it serves to perpetuate the traditional separation of clergy and laity which has its origins in the Middle Ages, not in the biblical early Church.

Having seen that God has given all believers equal status as priests, we need to see the outworking of that in a practical and realistic way. The more formal the church the harder it will be to implement, but if you have the vision for shared ministry it should be possible to make a start. Moses' father-in-law was wise enough to suggest to Moses that he didn't have to do everything himself! (Exodus 18·17–26). Part of today's problem is that people still feel they have to see *the* minister and be visited by him. As in Moses' case, that can create unreasonable pressure by the expectation of others. In Numbers 11 Moses once again faces the problem of the grumbling Israelites, and complains to God. 'The Lord said to Moses: "Bring me seventy of Israel's elders who are known to you as leaders and officials among the people. Make them come to the Tent of Meeting, that they may stand there with you. I will come down and speak with you there, and I will take of the

Spirit that is on you and put the Spirit on them. They will help you carry the burden of the people so that you will not have to carry it alone.' (Numbers 11:16–17 NIV).

'Then the Lord came down in the cloud and spoke with him, and he took of the Spirit that was on him and put the Spirit on the seventy elders. When the Spirit rested on them, they prophesied, but they did not do so again. However, two men, whose names were Eldad and Medad, had remained in the camp. They were listed among the elders, but did not go out to the tent. Yet the Spirit also rested on them, and they prophesied in the camp. A young man ran and told Moses, "Eldad and Medad are prophesying in the camp." Joshua son of Nun, who had been Moses' assistant since youth, spoke up and said, "Moses, my lord, stop them!" But Moses replied, "Are you jealous for my sake? I wish that *all* the Lord's people were prophets and that the Lord would put his Spirit on them!"' (Numbers 11:25–29 NIV).

Even two elders who were not there got the anointing! We can either react like Joshua and seek to limit the anointing to Moses or 'the leader', or like Moses and desire that everyone should be filled with the Spirit and move under the anointing of God.

Every church should have elders functioning, whatever you actually call them, (if anything). They have a shepherding role in the Body of Christ to lead the sheep into the greenest pasture and rescue them before they get damaged, or attend to their wounds if they do. Despite some of the excesses in managing the flock, shepherding is a biblical concept based on the Good Shepherd who laid down his life for the sheep, and should enable the flock to feed in peace and safety. Jesus has given us of His Spirit so that we may all function to our fullest potential in the Body of Christ, sharing the ministry and building up one another in the faith. May He alone be King.

2

The new wine is spilled

Mark 2:22

Most of the commentaries on Mark 2 emphasise that
wineskins which are not flexible burst and are ruined, but
forget that the wine is ruined too! We are dealing here with
the eternal and precious work and purposes of God
represented by the new wine of the Holy Spirit, and it is
indeed a tragedy if that new wine risks being spilled and
wasted, not only for the church concerned but for God
Himself. The Lord longs to pour out the new wine of
renewal into all the churches and individuals who will
receive it, but as Mark 2 states 'No-one pours new wine into
old wineskins'. In other words God will *not* pour out the
new wine of the Spirit where He knows for sure that it
cannot be contained and will not be received but merely fall
to the ground and be wasted. The metaphor or image used
here is deliberate, to indicate that there has to be flexibility
and adaptability to contain this active wine. The picture is
of it expanding and contracting as it settles down from
fermentation to maturity and stillness, and there is a certain
amount of activity with the Holy Spirit!

Man has always sought to bring everything under his
control, even the work of God. Everything is analysed,
categorised, theorised and turned into a doctrine. Even the
Holy Spirit has been changed from being a person to a

doctrine! Denominations develop out of the emphasis on one particular aspect of teaching and we end up being both inflexible and intolerant. This is seen in the development of the different denominations historically. Within one generation of the early Church being established all sorts of fasle doctrines had been introduced, and religious men had organised the work of God in the way they wanted, ignoring most of what the apostles taught them. It is not coincidental that most of the New Testament letters contain corrective teaching to combat these heresies. Indeed those who want an 'early church' need to be aware of the major problems which that church experienced, as the same seeds from which the errors grew are still around today. Nevertheless fundamentalist bible believers still stood out for the truth, and many paid the price with their lives. The Emperor Constantine did untold damage to the work of God by declaring that he would put to death anyone who wasn't a 'Christian'. If you were undecided it suddenly became much easier to decide, but because you were not born again of the Spirit of God through repentance and faith you merely became a part of the state religion. We now have 'Christian' countries on this basis including Great Britain. In a poll some years ago people from every country were asked 'Do you believe in God?' The country with the smallest percentage was Japan and next was *England* – a so-called Christian country! This just underlines the point that the name is quite misleading unless you are born again, so we now have 'born again Christians' to differentiate from the others! Over 50% of Americans claim to be born again and the term is now even being used to advertise the 1984 Volkswagen Golf, so we may have to go full circle and be called 'believers'. The kind of damage this does is particularly relevant to the Jews, who see a 'Christian' country as responsible for the Holocaust, and therefore have a deep suspicion of all Christians as a result.

Down through the centuries politics and religion merged together, particularly in the Roman Catholic Church, which developed into a world power with both a political and religious base. Fundamental Christianity was infiltrated by such doctrines as prayers for the dead (AD 300), veneration of angels (AD 375), exaltation of Mary (AD 431), purgatory (AD 593), the first pope Boniface (AD 610), canonisation of dead saints (AD 995), the rosary (AD 1090), transubstantiation (AD 1215), the adoration of the wafer (AD 1220), tradition declared to be of equal authority to the Bible (AD 1545) and so on. Nor is it limited to past history. We have the immaculate conception (AD 1854), the infallibility of the pope (AD 1870), Mary the Mother of God (AD 1931), the Assumption (rapture) of the Virgin Mary (AD 1950) and Mary declared to be the mother of the Church (AD 1965).

During the time up to the Reformation there were still bible believers holding on to the truth, and Martin Luther only acted as the catalyst that brought about the Reformation. In Britain the split was due to Henry VIII, but God used this to establish a more biblically based church. The Church of England really had a chance to start afresh, and I would commend to you the thirty-nine articles in the back of the Book of Common Prayer. The restatement of fundamentals brought fresh life to the Church and nation. Unfortunately the Church of England also became the established church and has suffered from being the state religion ever since. John Wesley was an Anglican minister, but was rejected by his own Church. The Baptists developed historically through the doctrine of believers baptism being a post-conversion experience, and yet Spurgeon was initially rejected and left. These are examples of the old wineskins not being able to handle the new wine of what God is doing, and that can happen all too easily when we settle down and are inflexible to the Spirit and to revelation God wants us to understand and apply in the Church. Many works start in the Spirit but end up in the flesh, and we are all potentially in the position where it could happen to us. We are all to some degree too rigid, too inflexible and too set in our ways, so the Holy Spirit moves on with those who will move until they too become too rigid. Tragically that has been the situation over the centuries with many waves of revival, and the empty chapels and churches stand as a warning to us. New groups are founded on some new aspect of the truth such as the authority of Scripture, holiness, believers baptism, church government, the Baptism in the Spirit, the priesthood of all believers, or whatever. All of these doctrines are fine and biblically based, but it is because of our rigidity that we fail to apply them and so the Holy Spirit moves on like the wind with those that seek to be in the move of the Spirit and at the forefront of what God is doing.

We need to be aware of the main causes of brittleness, and allow the oil of the Spirit to be rubbed in to soften us and make us supple. One of the main causes of brittleness is tradition. It is interesting to note that the Greek word for tradition 'paradosis' has the numerical value of 666 if the letters are counted numerically. The Greeks often added up words using the alphabet as a numbering system, and of course 666 is the number of Anti-Christ. Tradition is part of the spirit of Anti-Christ that John states is *already* at work on the earth. Anti not only means 'against' but 'other', and tradition projects a different Jesus. For example, traditional art does not show Him as a strong healthy man able to overthrow the money changers' stalls but a weak pale feeble Jesus, which is far from the truth. Next time you are in an art gallery or cathedral compare the biblical Jesus to what you see communicated. We acquire traditional ideas as we grow up, and these can be hard to shed. I like to think of Jesus as Daniel saw Him or indeed as He is described in Revelation 1: 'among the lampstands was someone "like a son of man", dressed in a robe reaching down to his feet and with a golden sash round his chest. His head and hair were white like wool, as white as snow, and his eyes were like blazing fire. His feet were like bronze glowing in a furnace, and his voice was like the sound of rushing waters. In his right hand he held seven stars, and out of his mouth came a sharp double-edged sword. His face was like the sun shining in all its brilliance' (Revelation 1:13–16 NIV).

The point about this is that our revelation of Jesus will affect our relationship to Him, and tradition can misrepresent Him to the world. The same is true of God the Father. He gave the Law as the best possible set of laws for Man to live under in a right relationship with Himself and other men, yet the Pharisees misrepresented God and added their own rules, even challenging Jesus! 'He replied, "Isaiah was right when he prophesied about you hypocrites; as it is written:

'These people honour me with their lips,
but their hearts are far from me.
They worship me in vain;
Their teachings are but rules taught by men.'

You have let go of the commands of God and are holding on to the traditions of men."' (Mark 7:6–8 NIV).

We must beware that what we do is not purely based on tradition. Because of passing phases people feel secure in the past, in history, in tradition and in stability. You have only to observe the outcry about tampering with the words of the National Anthem, Communion or Service Book to see the strength of feeling! This is not to deny or sweep away the good things from our past, but we need to be open, to be flexible, to have our hearts set towards the Lord and to desire to worship the Lord in Spirit and in Truth, not with vain repetition which effectively quenches the Spirit.

Secondly there is the question of doctrine and how we perceive biblical truth. We tend to fear that some new doctrine or revelation may be exaggerated or even not from God, particularly because of the increase in the cults. In case it may be some way-out extreme teaching that won't pass the test of time, we feel it's safer to stick to what we know, rather than thoroughly check it out biblically. After all, the founders of our denomination thrashed out doctrine years ago and it's all written down, so if it's not there it must be suspect! It is of course right to check everything against the word of God, but paradoxically it probably is there but no longer accepted or applied. Indeed if we all went back to the founding vision of our church or fellowship there may well be doctrines that need to be re-emphasised. The final arbiter has to be the Bible as the wholly inspired word of God, and if we are out of line then we have to change and cannot merely excuse ourselves by saying that a particular passage is no longer relevant to today.

Thirdly there is the fear of change, which many seem to find a threat. We do not all adapt well to new people, new ideas, new forms of worship or even new leadership. The good old days somehow seem better but they may not actually have been good at all! If you look at why a church does what it does the way it does it, the reason may be purely one of habit. People usually defend not changing by saying that it would upset the older members of the church, but these older members may well have been praying for years that change and renewal would come! Fear of change is a cause of rigidity and brittleness. There may well even be a preference for the old ways, and not everyone will want the new wine of what the Spirit is doing today. 'And no-one after drinking old wine wants the new, for he says, 'The old is better.' (Luke 5:39 NIV).

Here we have an interesting situation where the old is

preferred, and as long as peole say that the old is better they will reject the new. The key to this is to see what happened when the two wines were drunk at the wedding in Cana. The guests drank the old wine until it ran out. However when Jesus created the new wine and it was served up, they expected it to be worse and were astonished when of course it was far better. That is equally true today wher fear reacts against the new wine, but when people actually try it they discover that they have misjudged it and it is indeed far better than they have been led to believe.

The question now arises how we can receive the new wine of the Spirit and be open to all that God wants to pour into the Church. The answer comes from two sources: revelation from the Word of God and the prophetic ministry to the Church. We will cover prophecy in the next chapter as it is a key factor in the work of God, and He has always had prophets down through the centuries to bring the word of the Lord. Revelation from scripture is the other source. By revelation I mean truth taught by the Holy Spirit from scripture that is Spirit and Life and witnesses with your own spirit. Jesus actually said that we would know whether His teaching was from God or His own and indeed when Peter confessed that Jesus was the Christ Jesus replied: 'Blessed are you, Simon son of Jonah, for this was not revealed to you by man, but by my Father in heaven'. (Matthew 16:17 NIV).

The clearest passage on this is in 1 Corinthians 2 (emphasis mine) 'We have not received the spirit of the world but the Spirit who is from God, that we may *understand* what God has freely given us. This is why we speak, not in words taught us by human wisdom but in words *taught by the Spirit*, expressing truths in spiritual words. The man without the Spirit does not accept the things that come from the Spirit of God, for they are foolishness to him and he cannot understand them, because *they are spiritually discerned.*' (1 Corinthians 2:12–14 NIV).

In other words we have to receive our doctrine as spiritual revelation from the Word of God and not from hymns or anywhere else, including the natural mind. It is a question of source and authority, and we are to rightly divide the Word of Truth and to form our own view of what the passage is saying. Paul writes that each should be convinced in his own mind, and the Bible actually recognises that not all Christians will believe the same thing, such as what you can eat or what you can do on the Sabbath (Romans 14:5). Ephesians 4:3 exhorts us to *maintain* the unity of the *Spirit* until we *attain* the unity of the *faith* (Ephesians 4:13), in other words we should always seek to fellowship on the common ground we have in Christ until we come by revelation into all the truth of the Christian faith. Paul was not taught by any man and received all his revelations direct from the Lord. We may not be of the same spiritual standing but the principle is the same and God wants to reveal truths to us. Martin Luther received the revelation of justification by faith alone from reading the Bible, and he had probably read Romans 3:28 many times before the revelation came as fresh manna from heaven. We all need to be open to what the Holy Spirit is saying to the Church and be flexible enough to receive it as the Word of the Lord.

If we are genuinely seeking to apply everything the Bible teaches we are very much on the right track. The problem of course comes when biblical truth is only partially or selectively applied, or mixed with other input such as culture and tradition or wrong teaching. This happened to the early Church, and the message to the seven churches in Revelation was written as a warning to us. It was to the *Church* that Jesus wrote 'Behold I stand at the door and knock' (Revelation 3:20). The churches listed are all told that if they do not repent Jesus will remove Himself, and all are told 'He who has an ear, let him hear what the Spirit says to the churches'. (Revelation 2:7, 2:11, 2:17, 2:29, 3:6, 3:13, 3:22.) It is no less true of us.

None of those churches remains today, and the area (Turkey) is predominantly Muslem. The Jews thought they were eternally secure because of God's covenant with Abraham, and although God has not totally abandoned them and all the promises will one day be literally fulfilled when Jesus returns to the earth, they have nevertheless been cut off from what God planned for them and the Church has been blessed instead, but with the same warning: 'If some of the branches have been broken off, and you, though a wild olive shoot, have been grafted in among the others and now share in the nourishing sap from the olive root, do not boast over those branches. If you do, consider this: You do not support the root, but the root supports you. You will say then, "Branches were broken off so that I could be grafted in." Granted. But they were broken off because of unbelief, and you stand by faith. Do not be arrogant, but be afraid. For if God did not spare the natural branches, *he will not spare you either.*

'Consider therefore the kindness and sternness of God: sternness to those who fell, but kindness to you, provided that you continue in his kindness. Otherwise, *you also will be cut off.*' (Romans 11:17–22 NIV.)

The cutting off is the removal of the presence of Jesus from the church, and indeed that church may not even realise that this has happened. It is caused not only by a hardening of the heart but also by *unbelief* and the rejection of biblical truth. God the Father, Jesus the Son, (the living Word) and the Holy Spirit are all totally committed to the Bible being the revealed Word of God, and anyone who challenges the authority of scripture, even if born again, will face the consequences. For the unbeliever it will be judgement for committing the one unforgiveable sin, namely the rejection of Jesus as revealed in scripture. For the believer it wil be the shame of being called least in the kingdom of heaven.

'Anyone who breaks one of the least of these commandments and *teaches others to do the same* will be called least in the kingdom of heaven' (Matthew 5:19 NIV).

It is time that we took the Word of God as seriously as we should and asked the Holy Spirit to lead us into a greater depth of revelation from scripture, for without this there cannot be any genuine or lasting revival.

'*All* Scripture is God-breathed and is useful for teaching, rebuking, correcting and training in righteousness' (2 Timothy 3:16 NIV).

We need our hearts to be on fire with the Word, even as those who walked to Emmaus declared: '"Were not our hearts burning within us while he talked with us on the road and *opened the scriptures* to us?"' (Luke 24:32 NIV).

Without receptiveness to the Word of God there can be no true renewal of God's Church, for this is indeed one of the main areas that needs changing. God wants us to stand in awe of the Scriptures and to rediscover them as Josiah did in his day (2 Kings 22), otherwise we shall miss what the Lord wants to do among us. May His Church listen to what the Spirit is saying at this time.

3

Earnestly desire spiritual gifts
1 Corinthians 14:1

God gave spiritual gifts to the Church because He intended them to be used when believers met together as the Body of Christ. They therefore need to be considered in the context of our corporate life together. God never intended them to be a kind of special exclusive blessing for a select few while leaving the overwhelming majority of believers to struggle on their own. Indeed spiritual gifts have become a problem area for many churches precisely because Christians are receiving them: The Church in general has been so used to doing without them for so long that they are almost an intrusion, considered the result of fanaticism – extreme, and definitely not for use in church services. Instead of giving them their full and proper place in God's order they are often banished to the prayer meeting or restricted to private use only, with the hope that this will maintain unity and avoid conflict within the church. We are now living in days when God wants all the spiritual gifts restored to their proper biblical function, and churches are going to have to come to terms with what God is doing through the outpouring of the Spirit. The Holy Spirit *never* causes a division or split in a church on this issue. It is the inflexibility of the people to recognise and absorb what God is doing, and it is a corporate problem that needs to be faced

31

and tackled rather than seeking a cheap peace. There may be a separation as a result, because in any group there will be those keener than others to move on with God, but it is hardly God's fault if this happens. Indeed God wants us all to walk in the light and it is better to be honest and open and seek a solution rather than allow the devil to stir up rumblings of discontent anywhere in the Body of Christ.

Very few would disagree that spiritual gifts including tongues are for personal use in building up an individual believer and for ministering in counselling. The bigger issue is to what degree they should be used corporately in meetings and services. Much confusion arises over 1 Corinthians 12–14, so it is worth going over some basic ground at this point.

Firstly God does not want us ignorant about spiritual gifts (1 Corinthians 12:1) and the more you know and understand the better. Paul is thorough in his exposition to dispel ignorance not compound it! Let us look at those controversial gifts.

'But the manifestation of the Spirit is given to every man to profit withal.
For to one is given by the Spirit the word of wisdom; to another the word of knowledge by the same Spirit;
To another faith by the same Spirit; to another the gifts of healing by the same Spirit;
To another the working of miracles; to another prophecy; to another discerning of spirits; to another divers kinds of tongues; to another the interpretation of tongues;
But all these worketh that one and the selfsame Spirit, dividing to every man severally as he will.' (1 Corinthians 12:7–11 AV).

Many books are available which cover the gifts in detail but a brief summary of each is included here for clarity.

The word of wisdom is the gift of supernatural wisdom for a specific situation, so that you know you are receiving directly God's wisdom on the matter. It is a higher wisdom than the natural mind and comes from the Spirit of God as a gift. Usually you have to come to an end of natural wisdom first, but God gives it as a gift and in line with James 1:5 'If any of you lacks wisdom, he should ask God, who gives generously to all without finding fault; and it will be given to him.' This is a wonderful gift covering many situations.

The word of knowledge is the gift of a key to unlock a situation. For example God can reveal the cause of a problem in the past or reveal a need. As God knows everything He simply gives the knowledge needed for the situation. It can expose a sin, such as Ananias and Saphira secretly withholding money and lying about it. It is often used in healing meetings to instil faith that if God can reveal the sickness He can also heal the person who has it! It is invaluable in counselling and a necessary part of the Church's resources, as it enables you to hear direct from God.

The gift of faith is the special supernatural gift of faith for a situation beyond your own faith. God has given to *every* believer the measure of faith (Romans 12:3) so you have the normal measure. You then have to develop your faith to go from faith to faith, and faith comes from hearing and applying the Word of God (Romans 10:17). God will *never* move outside the realm of faith because 'Whatever is not of faith is sin' (Romans 14:23) and 'without faith it is *impossible* to please God' (Hebrews 11:6). Rather than have us move in unbelief God gives the gift of faith to enable Him to move in a situation beyond our own normal level of faith.

The gifts of healing are self-explanatory and cover both physical and emotional healing. This is healing in the name of Jesus through the power of the Holy Spirit, and although it is a gift to the church, i.e. primarily for believers,

God will often heal unbelievers as a sign to them that the gospel is true. There are many ways the gift can be given and received, and it is not restricted to healing meetings or any set formula. Divine health is a gift to the Body of Christ.

The working of miracles is the instant manifestation of the power of God, and should not be confused with healing, which may take time. The instantaneous cure of a sickness or the recreation of a part of the body is a miracle. It covers a wide area and is in essence the manifestation of the supernatural power of God in whatever way is needed. You work your own miracles by faith and often several of the gifts will work together. It is a marvellous gift from God and we should be grateful for it as well as all the other gifts. There may well come a time when you will have to move into this area and seek God for a miracle working ministry repeating many of the miracles that Jesus did.

Prophecy is simply speaking the pure word of God, not necessarily relating to the future. Often it is preceded by 'Thus saith the Lord', and those prophesying are bringing a message from heaven and are told to prophesy according to their faith. It is a much needed gift in the Body of Christ and we all should be hearing from the Lord and desiring to prophesy. It is not intended to be used for guidance but for the strengthening, encouragement and comfort of the Body of Christ (1 Corinthians 14:3).

The discerning of spirits is the ability to discern what is happening in the spirit realm. It covers knowing whether a prophecy or tongue is counterfeit and is therefore a check for the Body of Christ, and also links with the word of knowledge to discern what is happening spiritually. For example when Jesus said to Peter 'Get thee behind me Satan' he was exercising this gift, as Satan had manipulated Peter to divert Jesus from the will of the Father, and Jesus discerned the Satanic source.

Tongues are languages supernaturally given by the Holy

Spirit which have not been learnt. We know this from Acts 2 where 15 are listed as being heard on the day of Pentecost. They also include angelic languages (1 Corinthians 13:1). Some are known to God alone. The point is that they are not incoherent nonsense but actually communicate in the Spirit. As with learning a language you get a few words, then more and finally a flow, so it is with tongues and some are better at it than others. You can have more than one tongue or language, and can even ask God to add more! The reason God gives tongues from the Spirit is so that we move out of the natural area which we control into the Spirit area, which the Holy Spirit controls. Tongues therefore have a private function such as praying, for that is what praying 'in the Spirit' actually is, and a public function to speak out the tongue given from God *so that it may be interpreted*.

The interpretation of tongues then becomes obvious. You need people to interpret the tongues given publicly otherwise there is no point in having them. This too is a gift. It's an interpretation, not necessarily always a literal translation, so the length of the tongue and the length of the interpretation can differ.

The nine listed gifts of the Spirit are given to individuals for the *common good* (1 Corinthians 12:7 NIV). In that context, i.e. when believers meet together in the church service not everyone will manifest all the gifts including tongues as sheer numbers effectively make it impossible. Nevertheless Paul still desires that *all* should speak in tongues (verse 5). There clearly has to be a difference between speaking in tongues personally and giving a message in tongues in a meeting. Everyone should do the first but not everyone has opportunity for the second. In fact he says that only two or three at a time should do the second (verse 27). Once you see that difference the whole passage slots into place, and when the second reference is quoted be aware that it does not refer to an individual believer but a church meeting. Exactly the same principle applies to prophecy. We are particularly urged *'earnestly* to *desire prophecy'* in 1 Corinthians 14 verses 1, 5 and 39 which then means that we can give the word of the Lord, but as with tongues Paul expects everyone to prophesy privately and from time to time to use this gift as part of their public ministry. That is why not all prophesy in the meeting! Because a meeting needs to be decent and orderly Paul gives specific instructions on how it should flow. For example a tongue should be followed by an interpretation and if there isn't one you should seek one (1 Corinthians 14:13) otherwise it's better to keep quiet.

1 Corinthians 14:19 'But in the church I would rather speak five intelligible words to instruct others than ten thousand words in a tongue' is often quoted to defend the absence of tongues among the believers, despite Paul saying 'in the *church'* referring to a meeting, and verse 18 actually says 'I thank God that I speak in tongues *more than all of you'*!

God is a God of order and it is to avoid disorder and confusion that Paul gives the detailed instructions to the Corinthian church. The avoidance of the use of spiritual gifts is no real solution when difficulties arise and effectively prevents the Body of Christ functioning as God intended. There needs to be an opportunity for gifts and ministries to develop and if this cannot be in the main service or meeting then some other occasion needs to be found because this is how believers are built up and the Body of Christ grows.

You will now see how this ties in with the priesthood of all believers because body ministry is impossible without it. It is because we don't usually see all believers as priests that we do not have meetings based on that principle. One man cannot lead body ministry by definition. Whatever structure you currently have and however much you try to move towards a biblical model of leadership the crunch will come in the services or meetings. This is where it shows the degree you believe in body ministry and the ability of all believers to minister. To restate the principle on which body ministry functions: 'What then shall we say, brothers? When you come together *everyone* has a hymn, or a word of instruction, a revelation, a tongue or an interpretation. All of these must be done for the strengthening of the church.' (1 Corinthians 14:26.) In modern language it means that everyone has received something from the Lord and can give it at the meetings. Anyone can start a chorus, share a testimony, give teaching from the Bible, share a truth God has shown them, give a message in tongues, interpret someone else's tongue or give a prophecy. There then follows detailed instruction on how to keep the meeting in order. It is worth noting in passing that women are also priests automatically as far as God is concerned. The current debate about 'women priests' leading a church like a man is a challenge to the authority that God has clearly structured in 1 Timothy 2:12. They are not to have a teaching ministry nor authority over men, whatever the current sociological vogue, because Paul's argument is not based on culture but *creation*. As priests they should have equal opportunity to contribute in a meeting.

As far as the services are concerned the Holy Spirit has given each person something, whether they actually have the opportunity to share it or not. It should be possible to share it most of the time, and it is important to arrange the meetings so that this can happen, preferably without the 'leaders' at the front and the chairs all pointing towards them, which creates the expectation that they will be the ones who will be ministering. Full body ministry means letting the body minister to the Head, Jesus and to the other members.

Ideally you should have a group of less than 250 in number, all filled with the Spirit, and who have sought the

Lord before the meeting and *all* come prepared to share what they have. The meeting would be totally under the control of the Spirit to ensure that each person gives their contribution in order. Although not everyone will actively speak or start a chorus they are still equally part of the meeting, and there will be a theme, order and a progression of interrelated ministry. Of course you rarely have the ideal situation and there will be mistakes as people learn to minister. If in order to avoid this learning process and mistakes you never let the body minister you in effect deny the Holy Spirit the opportunity to build up everyone on the 1 Corinthians model and to reach out to the Lord to develop their ministry and speak prophetically to the church. You can for example opt for an intermediate stage where musicians lead the choruses and they come up on an overhead projector, followed by a planned speaker and a set subject. You can mix leadership from the front with corporate participation, but it helps not to have everyone pointing to the front, as it is not only hard to see who is speaking, but creates the expectation of ministry from the front and can inhibit more timid people from contributing. True body ministry means that the leaders will not necessarily speak anyway. We do need to give the Holy Spirit the opportunity to speak prophetically to the Church, and the instruction from Paul in this matter is: 'Quench not the Spirit. Despise not prophesyings. Prove all things; hold fast that which is good.' (1 Thessalonians 5:19–21 AV.)

Many leaders and churches fear that the meeting will somehow be out of control if they allow body ministry, because no-one is visibly in charge. This is not actually true, as the elders are invisibly supporting and watching over the meeting in a corrective role to prevent disorder, and the sign of a good meeting is that their presence is hardly noticed. It's not a free for all but freedom to minister, knowing that there is a safety net if needed. In

38

addition there are the biblical checks of discernment and weighing prophecy. There is also the basic witness of the Holy Spirit so that each person can filter out what is not Spirit and life. God is actually able to speak through His ministers, and the gifts of the Spirit such as tongues and prophecy are God speaking to the meeting. In an open meeting of this type you would expect choruses, prayer, prophecy, tongues, interpretation, singing in the Spirit, dancing in the Spirit and possibly words of knowledge and wisdom, healing or whatever the Lord directs, as He is directing the meeting. God wants us to worship Him in Spirit and in Truth and that may well involve us in moving into areas we are not naturally comfortable with.

The prophetic ministry is a key ingredient in body ministry. All through history God has raised up prophets to bring the word of the Lord to His people, despite its frequent rejection, and God wants this ministry in the Church today. In 1 Corinthians 12:28 God has appointed first apostles, (who by the way need to have those 'signs following' that mark an apostle such as signs, wonders and miracles (2 Corinthians 12:12) and not merely be sent out from their church) and second prophets. That is a measure of their importance, as the Church needs to hear the Word of the Lord and encourage all those with a prophetic ministry to go deeper. We must never despise prophesying, but rather weigh the prophecies against the Bible and exercise discernment and the witness of the Spirit. What is your own attitude to spiritual gifts? Do you seek them and earnestly desire to prophesy? If so ask the Lord and claim the promise of Luke 11:9 that you will receive what you ask for. The giver is more important than the gifts but God does want His Church fully equipped and for you to have them.

Before closing this chapter I would like to share the cautionary tale found in 2 Samuel 6. When the ark of the covenant was brought into Jerusalem David danced before the Lord with all his might. It was quite a sight!

'Michal daughter of Saul watched from a window. And when she saw King David leaping and dancing before the Lord, she despised him in her heart.' The chapter ends . . . 'And Michal daughter of Saul had no children to the day of her death.'

If you despise body ministry and God's principles for meeting together, tongues, dancing in the Spirit and even the gifts of the Spirit, the result will be the same – barrenness in your life and church. It is up to us to allow the Holy Spirit His perfect way with us and to submit to the word of God, so that we do not miss any of what God has for us in these days of renewal either as individuals or corporately as the Body of Christ. May we respond like David 'I will become even more undignified than this, and I will be humiliated in my own eyes.' (2 Samuel 6:22 NIV).

4

You err because you know neither the Scriptures nor the power of God

Mark 2:22

During these days of renewal and restoration it is of paramount importance that the Bible is given its recognition as the final source of authority, for without a return to fundamental biblical truth there can be no effective revival. The two foundational pillars, as stated by Jesus, are the scriptures and the power of God. Any person or church that denies either or both of these will inevitably flounder. There is currently an alarming move away from the Bible being the literal revealed Word of God, including in some evangelical circles, where it now merely 'contains' the word of God. If the Bible 'contains' the truth rather than 'is' the truth then any individual passage need not necessarily be literally true but merely contains a truth, possibly metaphorically or allegorically. For example the story of Jonah can be seen as allegorical and the big fish poetic licence. The story of creation itself need not be literally true but illustrative of a general principle that God was in charge of whatever time-span it took. The inevitable result of this is to question whether *any* passage is literally true as it need not necessarily be so. Major questions then arise, for example whether there will literally be a heaven and hell or the thousand year reign of Jesus on the earth that Revelation 20 refers to. It is an awesome responsibility to challenge anything in the Bible for two reasons. First of all Jesus Himself accepted the *whole* of the Old Testament as being literally true, including creation in six days, Adam and Eve, Jonah and hell being a physical place, as He specifically referred to all these during His ministry. In Mark 10, when questioned on divorce, Jesus replies in verse six that from the beginning of creation God made them male and female. Jesus did not believe that Man evolved from apes and taught both creation and a literal Genesis. There are nine places where Jesus referred to Jonah. The most direct is: 'For as Jonah was three days and three nights in the belly of a huge fish, so the Son of Man will be three days and three nights in the heart of the earth.' (Matthew 12:40 NIV.)

Let us consider the question of a literal hell. We should all have the fear of hell if we reject Jesus as Saviour and Lord and Jesus is quite straight about this: 'But I will show you whom you should fear: Fear him who, after the killing of the body, has power to throw you into hell. Yes, I tell you, fear him.' (Luke 12:5 NIV.) It is now becoming intellectually unacceptable to believe in a literal hell. Indeed when a well-known evangelist was recently asked on television a direct question on whether there was a literal hell with a literal fire and a literal worm he repeatedly avoided saying 'yes' even when the question was pressed again and merely said that we have to be serious about hell, but the flames were not necessarily like those we have in a living room fire. Jesus on the other hand was quite straight about hell including its real flames.

'It is better for you to enter life crippled than to have two feet and be thrown into hell. And if your eye causes you to sin, pluck it out. It is better for you to enter the kingdom of God with one eye than to have two eyes and be thrown into hell, Where

their worm does not die,
and the fire is not quenched.' (Mark 9:45–48 NIV.)

If there is no hell God has deceived us and is a liar, and if we cannot believe Jesus about hell then we cannot believe Him about anything else including our salvation. It is wholly out of character for God to misrepresent the truth and God is not a man that He should lie. The Bible is true, and if we disagree then we are the ones who are wrong.

During the last fifty years science has advanced so much that it has become the great infallible god. People believe that eventually Man will discover everything, including the origin of the universe, and be able to recreate life itself. Many Christians if faced with a choice would say that science is more accurate and more reliable than the Bible. They support the theory of evolution despite the strong evidence for life appearing suddenly on the earth, and say that the Bible was never meant to be a literal account of how life started anyway. Let us consider the case of Noah's flood. Prior to the flood the earth had a uniform climate. There had been no rain (Genesis 2:5) and because the mist acted as a kind of canopy the global temperature was uniform, which is why the stars were given to mark the seasons (Genesis 1:14). Scientists are now just beginning to discover this, and that a global flood rather than an ice age could have been responsible for the identifiable geological changes, yet still the Bible is felt to be inaccurate unless it agrees with science when really it should be vice versa. Evolution has been elevated from a hypothesis to the status of a proven fact. It is in fact a philosophy, because it presupposes that there is no creator God, and that given the right set of circumstances and enough time, (whatever that means), then life will appear. Science is basically fine (the word simply means knowledge) provided that we work from the evidence forwards and not from the conclusion backwards, looking for evidence to slot in conveniently, however much it has to be manoeuvred. If you had lived four hundred years ago you would have been assured that science had proved that the earth was flat, even though Isaiah writing several thousands years before Christ states that it is round (Isaiah 40:22). It's all a question of how much we know, and more and more scientists are now opting for the sudden life theory, although they may not be willing to call it creation because their model excludes the possibility of a Creator God. Christians must not accept science as a higher authority than the Bible, which will ultimately be proved correct, as has happened with much of the archaeological controversy over the dating of early historical events.

The Bible indicates that life started approximately six thousand years ago. There is enough chronological evidence in scripture to be quite accurate about this, but rather than considering the specific day, month, and year we will briefly look at the genealogies given and the principle in 2 Peter 3:8 that 'a day is as a thousand years.' The earth was not created in a random sort of way, for mankind to increase until some awful mistake happened and we blew up the earth with a nuclear explosion. God in His foreknowledge knew what Man would do and planned our salvation accordingly. If Man sinned in the Garden of Eden it would seem logical for the Saviour to come immediately to redeem fallen Man. God however had everything under control. 'You see, at *just the right time*, when we were still powerless, Christ died for the ungodly.' (Romans 5:6 NIV.)

God's timing was perfect. There is a day coming when the Holy Spirit will be removed from the earth in order for Antichrist to appear and rule. 'For the secret power of lawlessness is already at work; but the one who now holds it back will continue to do so *till he is taken out of the way*.' (2 Thessalonians 2:7 NIV.)

The point is that God determines the time when evil shall have free reign on the earth as part of the close of the age and it is not a random timing. The overall framework parallels creation. Just as there were six days of activity and one day of rest God wanted this established as a principle on the earth, which is why the Law of the Sabbath was given. There was not only to be one day's rest in seven, but also the land had one year's rest in seven as well (Leviticus 25). Every seven sevens, i.e. in year forty-nine they had the Sabbath year followed by a year of Jubilee. The principle of a day being a thousand years is part of the reason for the thousand year reign of Christ on the earth. That is precisely why Satan is locked up for a thousand years (Revelation 20:2), in order that the earth might have rest. Those that believe the Second Coming to be near are in fact saying that the six thousand years are almost over, by implication, based on 2 Peter 3:8, whether they realise it or not. That is the first reason why the Bible indicates the earth to be this age. We have in fact overrun it by a few years and are living in a period of grace. Time is actually up and God could close the six thousand years any time. It is only grace that has added on a few extra years so that more can be saved but this is not an open-ended extension of unlimited time.

The second indicator of the age of Mankind is the three genealogies listed in 1 Chronicles 1-8, Matthew 1 and Luke 3:23-38. These are written as historical records to establish the line from Adam to Jesus in an identifiable time framework and are more than a list of who begat whom! For example consider the order in God's oversight of history. 'Thus there were fourteen generations in all from Abraham to David, fourteen from David to the exile to Babylon, and fourteen from the exile to the Christ.' (Matthew 1:17 NIV.)

The most comprehensive genealogy is in Luke 3:23-38. The books of Kings and Chronicles give the detailed ages of the kings and are there as historical data.

The real point is that God is the God of order and history and the Bible can be considered an orderly historical record of life on the earth from creation to Jesus. Christians do not have to suppress reason, intellect and logic to accept Genesis 'by faith' alone, rejecting all their scientific training, but should recognise that God arranged for Moses to write an account of what happened, Jesus confirmed it and one day the evidence will too when enough is known. It is a wholly credible position first of all to acknowledge God as creator and secondly to believe in six day creation with the geological processes being condensed in time. Christians have been intimidated into feeling that belief in literal Genesis is like believing in Father Christmas – one day we'll stop believing in fairies and start believing in science!

Scientists are frequently wrong and revise many of their theories. God on the other hand *never* is and His truth will stand eternally. It's a question of who you choose to believe. The god of this world has blinded many minds and the father of lies has partially succeeded in deceiving even the elect. We have the witness of the Spirit that we are not the result of some freak circumstances in the atmosphere but that the Eternal God is our Father in heaven.

'And by him we cry, "Abba, Father." *The Spirit himself testifies with our spirit that we are God's children.*' (Romans 8:15–16 NIV.)

Once you are born again and have the indwelling Holy Spirit the idea of evolving from apes looks absurd.

Scientists continue to make pronouncements which the world stands in awe at, even though they may subsequently prove to be wrong.

It used to be said that it took millions of years to produce oil in the earth, but it can now be made in a matter of hours in a laboratory, and the National Coal Board is thinking of using the technique to turn coal into oil. We have allowed science to be exalted above God and this has affected Christians as well as everyone else. We need to place the Bible once again in its position as the supreme authority otherwise we shall be deceived and misled.

Any challenge to Scripture questions Jesus' integrity. The second reason why not to do this is because there are serious warnings to those who belittle the Word of God in these days of easygoing compromise. In Matthew 5 Jesus warns that those believers who teach other than biblical truth will be called least in the kingdom of God. It will be an eternal stigma and those that do this will have to give an account, but they won't of course lose their salvation. '"Do not think that I have come to abolish the Law or the Prophets; I have not come to abolish them but to fulfil them. I tell you the truth, until heaven and earth disappear, not the smallest letter, not the least stroke of a pen, will by any means disappear from the Law until everything is accomplished. Anyone who breaks one of the least of these commandments and *teaches others to do the same* will be called least in the kingdom of heaven"' (Matthew 5:17–19 NIV).

An equally direct warning is in Revelation 22: 'I *warn everyone* who hears the words of the prophecy of this book: If anyone adds anything to them, God will add to him the plagues described in this book. And if anyone takes words away from this book of prophecy, God will take away from him his share in the tree of life and in the holy city, which are described in this book.' (Revelation 22:18 NIV.) Although this specifically refers to the Book of Revelation it underlines how seriously God takes His Word.

Each believer has individual accountability, and therefore needs to know the Bible and receive personal revelation from it. This needs to be said because in the past the Bible has been a forbidden book to some, and churches have declared that only a priest may therefore interpret it, meaning the way the church wants. Whenever you hear people saying that a passage needs interpreting it generally means they want to change it from what it actually says to what they would like it to say! In some cases it has even meant amending the translation to create new words from the Greek rather than translate them, e.g. bishop, baptism which are transliterations as they would have caused embarrassment to the Establishment if translated literally. There are two areas in the scriptures that are currently under attack (apart from the usual attack on creation and heaven and hell). The first is the question of demons and their operation and the second is physical healing. Intellectualism, science and psychology have deceived many Christians into denying the reality of demons and therefore seeking help from doctors and psychiatrists rather than spiritual men with discernment. It is indeed tragic when people with spiritual problems that have all the hallmarks of demonic oppression write to Christian magazines for help and are then told to see a psychiatrist. Not only does this imply that problems are more likely to be psychological rather than spiritual, but also that Jesus or indeed the Church is incapable of meeting a person's need whereas a psychiatrist can! The scriptures refer repeatedly to demonic activity, and Jesus both discerned it and dealt with it. The inability of many churches to deal with this area reflects how urgently correct biblical teaching is needed to redress the balance. Because this ministry has been left to so few, deliverance is seen as a fringe activity practised by those who see a demon in everyone, and it is either avoided or rationalised away, with the result that someone genuinely oppressed is not taught how to get free and stay free, but is instead treated as being mentally ill in some way. I am not wanting to criticise the work of the medical profession in treating medical illnesses (I'm married to a doctor), but you cannot have a medical cure for a spiritual sickness. What we need in the Body of Christ is men with an awareness of principalities and powers prepared to minister deliverance in the name of Jesus to those whose problems are spiritual. We should not quench the liberating work of the Spirit in this area but rather seek to have the same ministry as Jesus:

> 'The Spirit of the Lord is on me,
> because he has anointed me
> to preach good news to the poor.
> He has sent me *to proclaim*
> *freedom for the prisoners*
> and recovery of sight for the blind,
> *to release the oppressed*,
> to proclaim the year of the Lord's favour.'
>
> (Luke 4:18–19 NIV)

Other books deal with the deliverance area in detail, but the point is that deliverance has not been replaced by psychology or drugs and the Church needs to be much more aware of its responsibility to be equipped to deal with it.

The second area concerns healing in the name of Jesus. This too was an integral part of Jesus' ministry to fulfil the Isaiah 61 prophecy about Him that He Himself quotes in the synagogue in Nazareth in Luke 4. The disciples were commissioned to heal, and it is included in the instructions of Mark 16, as indeed is deliverance.

> 'And these signs shall follow them that believe; In my name shall they *cast out devils*; they shall speak with new tongues;
> They shall take up serpents; and if they drink any deadly thing, it shall not hurt them; *they shall lay hands on the sick and they shall recover*.' (Mark 16:17–18 AV.)

The Holy Spirit is healing many people today in the name of Jesus, and we should all be seeking to be used by the Lord in healing under the anointing of the power of God, as Mark 16 does not suggest that these ministries are limited to a select few. There is however a tremendous amount of unbelief in this area that quenches the Spirit and blocks the healing flow of God. If Jesus could do nothing in Nazareth because of their unbelief (Matthew 13:58) the same will apply elsewhere. We need a revelation of the biblical basis for healing and of the power of God. Healing was provided in the Old Testament, for example through the serpent on the cross that Moses lifted up as a foreshadowing of Jesus (Numbers 21:9) as well as through the prophetic ministry of Elisha in response to prayers to the Lord. It was not however generally available in the way God actually wanted because Israel repeatedly violated the Deuteronomy 28 covenant and therefore came into the curses for disobedience, among which sickness is listed. Sickness is a curse as the result of sin, not just specific individual sins but the whole Fall of Man so it does not follow that the worst sicknesses affect the worst sinners or vice versa. All under the Adamic curse are vulnerable to sickness. If sickness came into the world after the Fall of Adam then the Second Adam, i.e. Jesus in redeeming us from the Fall also redeemed us from the consequences. In other words healing is included in the Atonement. If it was not then our salvation is incomplete. Some people discover divine healing in the Bible and then pray for the sick and see God heal, whereas others have been led of the Spirit to pray for the sick and then subsequently discovered from the Bible that it's normal! We need to see a limitless God who is able to do far more than we can imagine, and that it is we who have quenched the Spirit. If you don't see healing it is not because God is unwilling or unable, it is because it is not taught or applied in the Church with the result that it tends to be limited to healing meetings where an outside minister with a healing gift comes specially, or to certain Pentecostal denominations.

The point about this is that believers have the legal biblical right to health and healing, and should not accept sickness as something they have to put up with. We need to ask the Lord why we are sick and how He intends to heal us. It is not His will for anyone to be sick, but rather the consequence of the Fall. We all know we should be well and if we really believed it was God's will for us to be sick then it would be wrong for us to move out of His will and seek medical help. Often people have a passive fatalistic attitude that God's will is always done (it isn't), and therefore they are receiving all their circumstances including sickness from the hand of the Lord. God's will is that everyone should be saved, but clearly they are not. Just as salvation is conditional so is healing, and if we are in a right relationship with God and one another, have confessed our sins and move out in faith then God will meet us. Healing is a process that takes time and is not necessarily immediate. The Bible promises that we shall recover and gradually get better (Mark 16:18), but we have allowed the threat of failure or even apparent failure to prevent us from moving out in faith and praying for the sick. Not everyone will recover immediately, some possibly not at all, nevertheless we should still ask the Lord to heal them as an increasing proportion will recover, and it is fulfilling an important part of the ministry of the Church. When we see success and have the excitement of someone being completely healed, it builds up faith to continue to believe that Jesus is risen with healing in His wings. We need to see the power of God much more in this area.

One of the difficulties that many people experience is believing that the visible manifestation of the power of God is for today, especially if they personally have not seen God work in some dramatic supernatural way. The teaching is then wrongly seen as applying to the early Church only, which is course then questions the validity of any current

51

claims that God is moving in supernatural ways now. One particular passage is regularly quoted to imply that current 'moves of the Spirit' are not from God and bad exegesis of this passage can hinder the Holy Spirit's work. The passage is 1 Corinthians 13: 'Love never fails. But where there are prophecies, they will cease; where there are tongues, they will be stilled; where there is knowledge, it will pass away. For we know in part and we prophesy in part, but when perfection comes, the imperfect disappears.' (1 Corinthians 13:8–10 NIV.)

The argument put forward is that prophecies and tongues were used to help the early Church to get started but ceased when the full canon of scripture, i.e. the perfect, was revealed and the Bible as we now know it came together. The implication is that the gifts and ministries of the Holy Spirit were and are no longer needed, which is both untrue and damaging. Firstly, there is no evidence that prophecies and tongues did cease when the canon of scripture was formed, and even if it were true, what do we have now with their 'reintroduction' if they are no longer needed or valid? Some who support this doctrine would say that the current 'move of the Spirit' is counterfeit and a demonic deception. In fact the very reverse is the case, because the devil wants Christians to believe that all power and anointing ceased with the early Church, and therefore that there is nothing to appropriate, so it's pointless to ask God for spiritual gifts if they have been withdrawn.

Secondly there is the assumption that the Church does not need gifts and ministries of this kind now that we have the Bible instead. In fact we need the Bible *as well* as the filling of the Holy Spirit to be our source of strength and authority. The world needs to see a people clothed with power from on high, moving under the anointing of God, witnessing for Jesus with signs following.

Thirdly it assumes that the 'perfect' or 'perfection' is the full canon of scripture, which is not actually so. The perfect refers to heaven where God is Love and we will be with Him for eternity in perfect communion and fellowship in our resurrection bodies. We shall be like Jesus. We will have no need for tongues and prophecies then.

Finally the context of the 1 Corinthians 13 passage is right in the middle of Paul's exposition of the function of spiritual gifts and in the next chapter he goes on to talk about prophecy and tongues. He would surely have said something about their temporary use if this were the case. What has happened throughout history is a repeated rejection of supernatural gifts until they were so little in evidence that the Church assumed that they had ceased and taught so, with the error passed on down the generations.

It is awesome to label the move of the Holy Spirit as of the devil or counterfeit, as we are given the test of 1 John 4:1 'Test the Spirits'. John says that if you acknowledge the lordship of Jesus and His physical death and resurrection, you have the Holy Spirit and are not counterfeit. This check is there as a protection for the Church.

In many evangelical churches another doctrine is widely taught, namely that the baptism of the Spirit is an automatic part of salvation, based on the passage in 1 Corinthians 12:13 that we are all baptised by one Spirit into one body. We are of course all automatically placed in the Body of Christ at salvation, and all receive the Holy Spirit, otherwise we would not be Christians at all, but this is different from being baptised in the Spirit. If it was automatic then everyone would clearly be baptised in the Spirit and we would see the biblical evidence of it. I have often wondered why God did not do it automatically, and concluded that the answer lies with the 120 in the upper room at the time of Pentecost. There were many believers even after the death of Jesus, yet only 120 were sufficiently dedicated to be constantly in prayer and to have had the expectation that they would be clothed with power from on high, if they waited in Jerusalem as instructed. We too need to have the expectation, the obedience and the desire to be baptised in the Spirit and so God has not made it automatic but gives the empowering if we ask Him (Luke 11:13). Christians have been misled into assuming it was automatic which meant that there was nothing further to do, so no-one asked the Lord and both He and the Church missed out, with the result that the work of God is held up. The main point is to make sure that *we* have asked and received, whatever the Church teaches. It is those for whom this has not happened who tend to insist that it is automatic, whereas those who have been baptised in the Spirit say that for the vast majority it was a separate experience at a time other than their salvation. The Bible uses several different phrases which have been muddled and used interchangeably when they should not have been.

Firstly we need to distinguish between being *born* of the Spirit and *baptised* in the Spirit. Jesus Himself was born of the Spirit with God as His Father. God is Spirit and Spirit gives birth to Spirit (John 3:6). Jesus had the indwelling Holy Spirit right from birth and we of course do as soon as we are born again of the Spirit of God. Nevertheless Jesus did not begin His earthly ministry until He was clothed with power from on high at His baptism by John, when the Holy Spirit descended in bodily form like a dove. Something separate and specific happened at this point. Immediately after this Jesus is described in Luke 4:1 'Jesus, *full of the Holy Spirit*, returned from the Jordan.' Here we have a pattern which the disciples also followed. In John 20:22 Jesus breathed on them and said '*Receive* the Holy Spirit'. At that moment they received the indwelling Holy Spirit. Previously He had been *with* them but not *in* them (John 14:17). They were however told to stay in Jerusalem until they were clothed with power from on high (Luke 24:49) and received the baptism of the Spirit as a separate experience in both time and location. Acts 1:8 NIV puts it: 'But you will receive power when the Holy Spirit comes *on* you'.

We can therefore see three different stages for the disciples, and this is the pattern for us. The Holy Spirit is *with* us before conversion to convict of sin, righteousness and judgement and is omnipresent on the earth (John 16:8), but that does not mean we are saved unless we are born again. Certainly John 16 implies that the disciples had the Holy Spirit alongside them in a special way to direct their ministry to the world, but it is now the universal ministry of the Holy Spirit to convict all men that the gospel is true. You are only a Christian when stage two happens which is that you are born again and the Holy Spirit is *in* you and you are His temple (1 Corinthians 3:16). Finally you need the Holy Spirit to come *on* you and for you to be baptised in the Spirit and clothed with power from on high (Acts 1:8). That is the filling of the Spirit, which we need to maintain and live in constantly (Ephesians 5:18). The book of Acts demonstrates that the baptism in the Spirit is a separate experience. In Acts 8 Peter and John are sent to Samaria to follow the ministry of Philip who had preached the gospel. 'When they arrived they prayed for them that they might receive the Holy Spirit, because the Holy Spirit had not yet come *upon* any of them; they had simply been baptised into the name of the Lord Jesus.' (Acts 8:15–16 NIV.)

Those believers had self-evidently been saved and even baptised in water so if the baptism in the Spirit was automatic they would not have been prayed for. They would not have been baptised in the name of Jesus unless they were born again, so had the Spirit *in* them but not yet *on* them.

The same pattern is repeated in Acts 19 where they had been given the wrong baptism but were still believers in Jesus.

'. . . he found some disciples and asked them, "Did you receive the Holy Spirit when you believed?" They answered, "No, we have not even heard that there is a Holy Spirit." So Paul asked, "Then what baptism did you receive?" "John's baptism," they replied. Paul said, "John's baptism was a baptism of repentance. He told the people to believe in the one coming after him, that is, in Jesus." On hearing this, they were baptised into the name of the Lord Jesus. When Paul placed his hands on them, the Holy Spirit came *on* them, and they spoke in tongues and prophesied.' (Acts 19:2–7 NIV.)

If the baptism in the Spirit was automatic Paul would never have checked to make sure they had received. It would have been obvious! Many Christians are confused, and discover about baptism in the Spirit from scripture only to be told it's happened already without them knowing it! When it happens you will know, and if you're not sure whether it's happened to you or not seal it once and for all with the Lord by asking in faith according to the promise of Luke 11:13.

We all need to be sure that we know the scriptures and the power of God and not be deceived about our standing before the Lord, like those described in 2 Timothy 3:5 having a form of godliness but *denying its power*. The Laodicean church, which some consider to typify the last phase of the Church on the earth, said about itself: 'I am rich; I have acquired wealth and do not need a thing.' (Revelation 3:17 NIV.) Some say they have the Bible, they have preaching, they see people saved and indeed they are a live church. Even with this it is possible to be pitiable, poor, blind and naked. These four descriptions are how Jesus saw them:

Pitiable: Churches that claim to be live do not always have any real life in the Spirit. There may be plenty of activity, but how many are at the Bible studies and prayer meetings? Is there more reliance on natural resources, methodology and technique than the Holy Spirit? There is an appearance of wealth but Jesus considers it pitiable. What a pity to miss out on all the blessings God has for those who walk in obedience and truth. We need to stop measuring just numbers and work for real depth, stability and maturity.

Poor: The church said 'I am rich' but in what? God is not interested in money, expensive multi-use buildings, programmes or activities even though they have their proper place, but in men who will act as ambassadors for Jesus filled with the Holy Spirit. The goal is to present each man mature in Christ and to train men in their ministries who will make disciples for the Lord. There should be a quality of life in the Spirit among believers committed together to the Lord first and His work second. We need to be sure that we have the right kind of spiritual wealth among us that comes from having laid up much treasure in heaven.

Blind: We need to take a good hard look at ourselves occasionally and ask God to let us see things the way He does. We must not turn a blind eye to valid criticism but acknowledge our weaknesses and ask the Lord to deal with them. We need to see how totally dependent we are on the Holy Spirit and that we need His power and enabling in all we do. Often things look fine, and we simply do not see that Jesus is being squeezed out of His rightful place. May the Lord open our eyes.

Naked: God wants us to be clothed in holiness and righteousness. Sin robs us of this covering as in the Garden of Eden and we cannot conceal our true nakedness from God. It is like the story of the emperor's new clothes.

Everyone could see that he was naked except himself, as he had been deceived into believing he was clothed. God sees us as we really are and in some cases it is completely naked with no covering at all.

Revelation 3 is not all negative because Jesus offers them refining and true gold to be spiritually rich, white clothes to wear (the robe of righteousness) and salve to give spiritual insight. The Laodicean church thought Jesus was central to their ministry but He was in fact outside knocking to try and get in (Revelation 3:20)! Some of the harshest words of Jesus were for the official priests, the ministers of His day, for preventing the people from entering into the kingdom and giving them tradition instead of truth. Tradition and religion can be real enemies to the true work of God and we need to be aware how they can usurp the lordship of Jesus and deny the power of the Spirit. We must live by the scriptures and experience the power of God in our homes and churches.

5

Where there is no vision the people perish

Proverbs 29:18

Ever since the creation of the world God has had an eternal plan for mankind, including his salvation and eternal destiny. God wants every person on the face of the whole earth personally to receive Jesus into their hearts and lives as the one who died for their sin, so that they are made righteous by faith and are born again of the Spirit of God. In other words it's God's will for everyone to be saved and meet Jesus as Saviour rather than Judge. In addition to our salvation God has other objectives, the chief one being that we should be like Jesus who is the firstborn of many and not ashamed to call us His brothers. Although that process will be completed in the twinkling of an eye when we meet the Lord, God nevertheless wants it to start now on the earth. Not only are we to be Christlike in what we say and do, we should be continually filled with the Holy Spirit (Ephesians 5:18) so that the resurrection life within us overflows. We are ambassadors from another world and kingdom as our home is in heaven, therefore we should seek to fully represent Jesus in every aspect of His ministry. God no longer considers us servants or slaves but *sons* and *friends* (John 15:15). It is truly wonderful to have a revelation of Jesus as your friend who sticks closer than a brother (Proverbs 18:24) and to know that He is our brother as well as the Head of His body, the Church. The point is that we should have a much greater vision for the Church than merely seeing people saved and even growing as believers. We are being trained as sons for the Millenium and for eternity, as we shall see shortly.

'The Spirit itself beareth witness with our spirit, that we are the children of God: And if children, then *heirs*; heirs of God, and *joint*-heirs with Christ; if it so be that we suffer with him, that we may also be glorified together. For I reckon that the sufferings of this present time are not worthy to be compared with the glory which shall be revealed in us. For the earnest expectation of the creature waiteth for the *manifestation of the sons of God.*' (Romans 8:16–19 AV.)

The NIV translates verse 19: 'The creation waits in eager expectation for the sons of God to be revealed'. This is the key to what God is doing in our lives. Not only did Man fall with Adam but the *whole* of creation. That is actually why animals eat each other. It is not natural for animals to be carnivorous because God specifically made them vegetarian, and they did not eat each other before the Fall.

'And to *all* the beasts of the earth and *all* the birds of the air and *all* the creatures that move on the ground – everything that has the breath of life in it – I give *every green plant* as food.' (Genesis 1:30 NIV.)

This is of course why the lion will eat straw like the ox in the millenium (Isaiah 11:7) because during that period Jesus reverses the curse. This happens when the manifestation of the sons of God takes place when Jesus returns to the earth, but the process of making us into sons is starting now, including the discipline that goes with it (Hebrews 12:5–6). God's purpose is the restoration of all that was lost at the Fall and that we, that is the Body of Christ, should reign with Christ over creation in the same way that Adam originally did and for this to happen on the earth, which was created as the perfect environment for Man. Many Christians completely misunderstand the purpose of the Millenium and have a limited concept of this life and heaven, with little realisation that their time in heaven may be shorter than they thought! For those who are raptured they will only be there for seven years during the Great Tribulation. They will then return with the Lord to the earth.

Jesus could quite easily have left the Church in heaven with the Father while He personally reigned on the earth for a thousand years but He wants *us* with Him. Apart from this being specifically stated in Revelation 20:6 'they will be priests of God and of Christ and will reign with him for a thousand years' it is alluded to in such passages as Luke 18:29 which has a double meaning: '"I tell you the truth," Jesus said to them, "no-one who has left home or wife or brothers or parents or children for the sake of the kingdom of God will fail to receive many times as much *in this age* and, in the age to come, eternal life."' (Luke 18:29– 30 NIV.) This is partly fulfilled through the nature of the Body of Christ but will also happen in the Millenium. This also makes sense of the parables such as the parable of the talents. When Jesus says 'Because you have been trustworthy in a very small matter, take charge of ten cities' (Luke 19:17 NIV) He means it literally. The degree and extent of our rulership will depend on the faithfullness with which we look after what God has entrusted to us now. It is not just a nice parable to make a point but has prophetic meaning. Paul also includes this preparatory instruction in his letter to Timothy: 'exercise thyself rather unto godliness. For bodily exercise profiteth little: but godliness is profitable unto all things, having promise of the life that now is, and of *that which is to come*.' (1 Timothy 4:7–8 NIV.) This is not a reference to heaven but an age which is to come, and even if it did refer to heaven the principle would still be valid that what we do now on the earth affects us in the future more than we realise.

As far as vision is concerned we need a greater vision of God's eternal plan, His prophetic timetable and our current function here on the earth. We need to see our aim as being to present each man mature in Christ (Colossians 1:28) trained in godliness, and a good steward of all that has been entrusted to him (or her). In other words our vision for the Body of Christ must extend beyond salvation and sanctification to embrace God's wider purpose of making us sons to reign with Christ and to be part of the restoration of the earth to the original purpose of God. This is in fact why there will be a new heaven and a new earth as part of the Eternal State (Revelation 21:1) because God needs both. Earth is the perfect environment for Man so God will create a new one to fulfil that purpose at the close of the age. If this all seems too vast to grasp then your vision of God is limited. The fact that God has revealed these things to us in the Bible means that we should have that wider vision and let it thrill us.

'Eye hath not seen, nor ear heard, neither have entered into the heart of man, the things which God hath prepared for them that love him. But God hath *revealed them unto us by his Spirit*.' (1 Corinthians 2:9–10 AV.)

Hosea 4:6 declares 'My people are destroyed through lack of knowledge'. Our starting point therefore has to be to know that to which God has called us in Christ and to aim towards it. Where there is no corporate vision for the people it can be very hard to motivate them to press on with God particularly if they are experiencing trials and testing and not counting it all joy! (James 1:2). Peter writes that we should not be near-sighted or have short term goals but far-sighted or in other words have a vision that will make us effective and mature: 'make every effort to add to your faith goodness; and to goodness, knowledge; and to knowledge, self-control; and to self-control, perseverance; and to perseverance godliness; and to godliness, brotherly kindness; and to brotherly kindness, love. For if you possess these qualities in increasing measure, they will keep you from being ineffective and unproductive in your knowledge of our Lord Jesus Christ. But if anyone does not have them, he is *nearsighted* and blind, and has forgotten that he has been cleansed from his past sins.' (2 Peter 1:5–8 NIV.) It requires both vision and effort to achieve this. Paul likens it to training for a race where the prize is really worth winning: 'Run in such a way as to get the prize. Everyone who competes in the games goes into strict training. They do it to get a crown that will not last; but we do it to get a crown that will last forever.' (1 Corinthians 9:25–26 NIV.) We need to see that all that we are doing here on the earth does have a purpose and nothing we do for the Lord is ever wasted. May the Lord give us a vision for His work on the earth that stirs us to press on into that to which He has called us.

Once we have the vision we need to invest our faith and believe that God who has begun a good work in us will bring it through to completion if we co-operate with the Holy Spirit. If we are not in faith the vision will soon fade and we risk missing it. Within the broad context of presenting each man mature in Christ some will have the vision for evangelism, some pastoring, some teaching, some healing, whatever aspect of ministry it may be. That is why the ministries are established in the Body of Christ. They are there to fulfil the vision. 'It was he who gave some to be apostles, some to be prophets, some to be evangelists, and some to be pastors and teachers, to prepare God's people for works of service, so that the *Body of Christ may be built up* until we all reach unity in the faith and in the knowledge of the Son of God and *become mature*, attaining to *the whole measure of the fulness of Christ*.' (Ephesians 4:11–13 NIV.)

If you are willing to accept that this should be the vision for the Body of Christ then you also need to see that God's method of bringing it about is these specific ministries. Part of our vision for a Holy Spirit led church has to be to see these ministries established and functioning correctly, based on the biblical model which recognises the priesthood of all believers and the corporate participation required. It is the leaders' role to state the vision clearly and if necessary to write it down. 'Write down the revelation and make it plain on tablets so that a herald may run with it. For the revelation awaits an appointed time; it speaks of the end and will not prove false. Though it linger, wait for it; it will certainly come and will not delay.' (Habakkuk 2:2–3 NIV.)

It is because it will take time and may not be immediate that it needs to be there to refer to at a point of wavering if the church subsequently becomes unsure about its direction. It is up to each church or fellowship to seek God both about the vision and its application, so that all the believers are united about it, and are in faith together to see it come to pass.

Before closing this section on vision we need to note Luke 5:38 'No, new wine must be poured into new wineskins. And no-one after drinking old wine wants the new, for he says, "The old is better."'

As long as some people prefer the old and consider it better they will not make way for the new. They consider traditional historical Christianity structured through conventional one-man leadership within the denominations to be better.

The marriage at Cana can be seen as a picture of the Church. The guests thought that the wine they were drinking first was the best but once they actually ran out of their supply Jesus was there with His. When they tasted it they discovered the opposite of what they expected. It was in fact the best wine they had ever drunk, but they would never have done so if they had not run out of their own. The new wine of the Spirit is much better, but if you are used to the old and prefer it you may not want the new and will simply reject it as too new and lacking maturity. Sometimes your supply has to run dry before you find Jesus there with His, and you then discover that it is far better than you thought. We all need our wineskins to be flexible enough to receive the new wine of the Spirit and to desire it as God's best provision for the Church. May we prove what David wrote: 'Taste and see that the Lord is good.' (Psalm 34:8 NIV.)

Part II

How we quench the Spirit in our individual lives

Introduction

As we have seen God's purpose for the Church is to function fully as the Body of Christ here on the earth in biblical order, both in order to represent Jesus and to bring each believer into maturity as a son. For this to happen corporately each member of the Body of Christ needs to be full of the Holy Spirit and walking in the Spirit. We need to define more precisely what is meant by this, to avoid misunderstanding or confusion. All believers in the Body of Christ are first class citizens but all are clearly at different stages of growth, and as we look at these it is important for those at early stages of growth to press on rather than in any way consider themselves to be second class citizens.

First of all every believer 'has' the Holy Spirit by definition, otherwise he would not be saved (Romans 8:9). If you are born again of the Spirit of God according to John 3, you have the Holy Spirit permanently indwelling you and in order to seal it God has given us a guarantee!

'He anointed us, set his *seal of ownership* on us, and *put his Spirit in our hearts* as a deposit, *guaranteeing* what is to come'. (2 Corinthians 1:22 NIV.) We are bought with a price and belong to the Lord forever. When Jesus breathed on the disciples they received the indwelling Holy Spirit just as we do. Up to that point they had the Holy Spirit with them but not actually in them.

As we saw earlier Jesus did not begin His ministry until He was clothed with power from on high or baptised in the Spirit. It may seem odd that God should do this to Jesus particularly as John the Baptist says that Jesus will baptise us with the Spirit, but the baptism of Jesus by John had two purposes. The first was of course for Jesus to identify Himself with Man as He was to die as a man, but the second purpose was for the power of God to come on Jesus to fulfil His ministry. This is the experience of empowering and it is a pattern for us. Jesus is described as '*full of the Spirit*' in Luke 4:1, and Luke 4:14 states specifically: 'Jesus returned to Galilee *in the power of the Spirit*.' (Luke 4:14 NIV.)

Whatever you actually call it Jesus received power and anointing before starting His ministry that happened separately from being born of the Spirit, and therefore having the Holy Spirit right from conception. That in no way implies that Jesus was lacking anything in His divinity but it was the way God chose to do it, with the Holy Spirit descending in bodily form as a dove. It happened this way for the disciples as well and we should expect the same.

In Ephesians 5:18 Paul writes to a church that has been flagging and failing to grasp all the blessings they have in Christ, telling them 'Be filled with the Spirit.' This is perhaps the most confusing phrase which is the present continuous tense of the verb pletho, which simply means to make full. In other words Paul says that they should be continuously be being filled up with the Spirit. The best illustration is that of a glass. The empowering or baptism of the Spirit is the initial filling up by God and then as we pour out (or even get drained) then we need to be filled up again with the power of God. This is particularly important as this is where we should be aiming and the question for each of us is whether we are filled with the Spirit as it's possible to be baptised in the Spirit but not *filled* with the Spirit! We therefore have several stages, firstly to be born of the Spirit, then to be baptised in the Spirit and finally to be continuously filled with the Spirit.

Some Christians only ever experience the first stage, but even that brings you into abundant blessing and you can of course be used of God in preaching and teaching and many other ministries. More and more people are now discovering stage two as a living reality and they can then *in addition* move in the gifts of the Spirit and expect to see the dynamic power of God in their lives. A few actually live constantly filled with the Spirit as this is a great deal harder and means putting to death the old life and habits, and being totally reliant on walking in the Spirit and the power of God. It is God who gives us new life and the Holy Spirit out of love and grace, based on our repentance and faith in the Lord Jesus. It is on that basis that we can ask for the gift of the Holy Spirit according to Luke 11. We know that this refers to the baptism of the Spirit because it refers to us as sons who are already born again, as the gift is to the *sons* of the Heavenly Father, in other words believers.

Being 'filled' or full of the Holy Spirit is paradoxically up to us although it cannot of course happen unless God does it. It is up to us to be free enough to allow Him to have every part of us including the will and the emotions, i.e. the Soul. The Word of God divides between that which is soul and that which is spirit (Hebrews 4:12) separating the natural from the spiritual. To be filled with the Spirit means that God has 100% control, and our free-will allows us to deny Him that total control if we resist or quench the Spirit.

Before we are saved we are slaves to sin, which is our

master. It controls our innermost being and we obey it. Once we are saved this law is broken and we are freed from the compulsory will to sin for God has put a new law in our hearts enabling us to obey Him.

'So, my brothers, you also died to the law through the body of Christ, that you may belong to another, to him who was raised from the dead, in order that we might bear fruit to God. For when we were controlled by the sinful nature, the sinful passions aroused by the law were at work in our bodies, so that we bore fruit for death. But now, by dying to what once bound us, we have been released from the law so that we serve *in the new way of the Spirit*, and not in the old way of the written code.' (Romans 7:4–6 NIV.)

We are now no longer under the law of sin and death but the law of the Spirit of life (Romans 8:2). Earlier in Romans 6:14 Paul reminds us that sin shall no longer be our master and we should count ourselves dead to it. The point is that we have a choice whether to walk in the old ways of the sinful nature or the new way of the Spirit. It's either the old by the flesh or the new by the Spirit.

'It is for freedom that Christ has set us free. Stand firm, then, and do not let yourselves be burdened again by a yoke of slavery.' (Galatians 5:1 NIV.)

'You, my brothers, were called to be free. But do not use your freedom to indulge the sinful nature; rather, serve one another in love.' (Galatians 5:13 NIV.)

'But if you are led by the Spirit, you are no longer under law.' (Galatians 5:18 NIV.)

Paul then contrasts the works of the flesh and the fruit of the Spirit, showing what is the result of each type of life. God clearly wants us to be fruitful, but it remains up to us whether we will allow the heavenly gardener to prune and tend us so that we become Christlike. It is possible to be full of the Holy Spirit if we put off the old and put on the new.

'You were taught, with regard to your former way of life,

to *put off your old self*, which is being corrupted by its deceitful desires; to be made new in the *attitude* of your minds; and to *put on the new self*, created to be like God in true righteousness and holiness.' (Ephesians 4:22–24 NIV.)

The Holy Spirit is given without measure (John 3:34) so we have in potential the measureless power of the Spirit living inside us and we need to submit to His rulership in every area. The Holy Spirit can be resisted (Acts 7:51), quenched (1 Thessalonians 5:19), grieved (Ephesians 4:30), tempted (Acts 5:9), and insulted (Hebrews 10:26–29). This section seeks to help believers to allow the Spirit to work freely and to cover those areas where we can so easily quench the Spirit and deny ourselves the experience of truly being led by the Spirit of God.

6

You cannot serve God and mammon

Luke 16:13

We live in a world of competition, ambition and ever increasing wealth, at least for those in the industrialised western societies. If you cannot make it to the top of the ladder and be successful through ability then there is always the possibility that you might win the pools or your premium bond could just come up. The hope is at least always there in your dreams. You work for a new car every two years, foreign holidays and of course an inflation-proofed pension. You are assessed socially by your income and occupation and if you happen to be a Christian might even consider this to be the blessing of the Lord. After all Abraham was rich, so was Job and 'the blessing of the Lord maketh rich'! Before you realise it you are caught up in the world's system of values and the love of money which is the root of all evil. The uncomfortable truth is that many of us would really like it both ways, to have treasure in heaven but also to live in comfort and ease on the earth!

'"Watch out! Be *on your guard* against all kinds of greed; a man's life does not consist in the abundance of his possessions."

'And he told them this parable: "The ground of a certain rich man produced a good crop. He thought to himself, 'What shall I do? I have no place to store my crops.' Then

72

he said, 'This is what I'll do. I will tear down my barns and build bigger ones, and there I will store all my grain and my goods. And I'll say to myself, "You have plenty of good things laid up for many years. Take life easy; eat, drink and be merry."'

But God said to him, 'You fool! This very night your life will be demanded from you. Then who will get what you have prepared for yourself?'

This is how it will be with anyone who stores up things for himself but is not rich towards God."' (Luke 12:15–21 NIV.)

After telling this parable Jesus goes on to talk about not worrying about food and clothes but to seek *first* His Kingdom and trust God for all His provision. If you are locked into your own provision it will prevent you from seeking first God's, because you will be unable to be in faith to break free from the demands of the system, e.g. the mortgage, rates, electricity, gas etc..

The area of money has to be faced and dealt with for every Christian, because it is a major snare that prevents many from seeking the Kingdom of God or even doing God's work. The starting point has to be Genesis. Before Adam sinned the garden just grew and flourished with abundant fruit of every kind, and Adam quite effortlessly enjoyed God's wonderful provision and fellowship. When God pronounced the curse after the Fall, He spoke first to the serpent whose curse was to crawl and eat dust, secondly to Eve whose curse was increased pain in childbirth and lastly to Adam whose curse was that the ground would no longer willingly yield its produce. He would have to work.

'Cursed is the ground because of you:
Through painful toil you will eat of it all the days of your life.
It will produce thorns and thistles for you,

and you will eat the plants of the field.
By the sweat of your brow you will eat your food
until you return to the ground, since from it you were
taken;
for dust you are and to dust you shall return.'

(Genesis 3:16–19 NIV.)

All those with a job know something of having to sweat it
out with sheer hard work whether serving an
apprenticeship, being an articled clerk or the early days of
getting a business established. It's not restricted to
gardening! At the Fall work became a curse, and we need
both to see this and God's answer. There is no work in
heaven, and Jesus did not work to earn a living during His
ministry. Because He has redeemed us from the Adamic
curse, God has done something wonderful for every
believer, and turned our cursing into blessing. In other
words the work we now do is not for income and food, but
as unto the Lord, whatever it be. We can now pray for and
expect God's blessing on our work if we walk in obedience
to Him. This is meant to be a liberating revelation, because
the whole reason and basis for work has changed. We no
longer *have to* work because of the curse; we can now do
whatever God wants and trust Him to meet our needs
according to His riches in glory.

'And my God will meet all your needs according to his
glorious riches in Christ Jesus.' (Philippians 4:19 NIV.)

It is important to see this because if you are still serving
the system (mammon) you will be concerned about your
mortgage and pension and how you will make ends meet if
you give it all up to serve the Lord. God sees it quite
differently, and indeed it should all have been given up
anyway at salvation, in the sense of it being handed over to
the Lord. God sees it as a change from working for Him in
an office in London to working for Him in a hospital in

74

India. If your supply comes from Him and you are in faith, then it makes no difference. It if comes from the monthly paycheck then of course it does! God may well wish to provide for you in that way and does so for millions of believers, but it is *He* who provides and not the system. Work should be a blessing serving the Lord and if it seems a grind you need to see yourself working for Him. It should make no difference if you are made redundant because God may well use these very circumstances to move you on to the next job He has for you, whether salaried or not. You need to determine that you will serve the Lord in whatever area of work He calls you to, whether well-paid or not and trust Him to meet your needs. This then frees you to do what He wants joyfully. You need your husband or wife to agree that God will set your standard of living whatever it is, because God wants you in unity and faith together. Wives have been known to press their husbands to earn more (!) and it is unfair pressure on any man. They should learn to be content with what they have. Godliness with contentment is great gain (1 Timothy 6:6).

In relation to being led of the Spirit in the area of money the crunch comes on giving and stewardship. If you are serving mammon you will instinctively dislike giving, and tithing even more! Although we are no longer under law and therefore not biblically instructed to tithe – nowhere in the New Testament are we told to – it is nevertheless a good rule of thumb if only because Abraham gave a tenth to Melchizedek in Genesis 14:20, and Jacob promised a tenth to God in Genesis 28:22, both before the law was given. For some people that would be too much and for others far too little. That is why we must be led by the Spirit of God as to how much of *His* money that He has lent us we should transfer to a different steward. Giving needs to be through free-will, in secret and in faith. Our willingness to be open to the Spirit in giving is a good measure of whether we feel we need to hang on to 'our' money because we fear that rainy day will come. We must also respond to the Holy Spirit and not always to an apparent need. For example a need may be caused by bad stewardship and squandering and God may first want to teach good stewardship before providing more money. God may possibly want a large sum accumulated for some purpose. Of course the principle in James of works going hand in hand with faith remains true, but the key is always to hear from God and if you are married expect God to tell your partner the same figure, so you're sure it really was that amount! Unfortunately the worldly attitude to money has affected the Church, so that appeals are constantly made for this or that ministry, rather than serving the Lord and praying it in. It is quite reasonable to make needs known but the key is to be in faith and look to God rather than how to fundraise. This may seem obvious, but there have been cases of professional fund-raising companies being hired to bring in the money! It is a question of motive, and the Church can forfeit its credibility if it is perceived as interested in money and buildings rather than people and ministry. We must never allow our attitude to other believers to be affected by their financial status (James 2:1–4) – i.e. if a person is rich then he's the chap to run the church finances! When Samuel chose David he thought all the other sons of Jesse looked the part, but he was led by the Lord to David as God looks on the heart, not the outward appearance, and so must we, as looks are very deceptive.

'Do not love the world or anything in the world. If anyone loves the world, the love of the Father is not in him. For everything in the world – the cravings of sinful man, the lust of his eyes and the boasting of what he has and does – comes not from the Father but from the world.' (1 John 2:15–16 NIV.)

In the area of stewardship we need to beware of the

potential snares that could draw us away from being free to do what God wants. The first of these is straight worldliness, the cravings of sinful man and the lust of his eyes. We must consciously and deliberately reject the world system of materialism and gathering more and more of the world's goods that are ceaselessly promoted. The key to good stewardship is to ask God about everything, which house to buy, which car if any, which clothes and indeed if it is genuinely His money we are spending then we must be willing to take no for an answer on some things. The issue is not that 10% or so is God's and the rest is ours. This will deceive you into thinking you can spend the 90% how you choose! Mammon is a very powerful magnet to beware of.

"'Therefore come out from them and be separate,
says the Lord.
Touch no unclean thing,
and I will receive you."
"I will be a father to you,
and you will be my sons and daughters,
says the Lord Almighty."' (2 Corinthians 6:17–18 NIV.)

The second snare in serving God is ambition, or to be 'successful'. We need to see that we are liberated from any kind of competition in Christ and that promotion comes from the Lord. He raises men up and deposes others. Throughout the Bible this has been God's way – with Joseph, Moses, David, Daniel and many others, so if we work as unto the Lord and are promoted then it's up to Him. Ambition can be a problem in the Body of Christ, with men ambitious to be well-known platform speakers or to run churches or fellowships, be elders or deacons etc.. Of course it's valid to seek to serve God as an elder (1 Timothy 3:1) provided it's serving God and the Body, and not self-seeking for position. It can be a snare even in the work of

God, and we should not be seeking status either in the Body of Christ or the world, but rather allowing God to determine our role and position. 1 Corinthians 4:13 shows how the early believers were considered the scum of the earth, as rubbish, and Hebrews 11 talks about them wandering the earth as rejected men but full of the glory of God.

The third snare in serving God is the natural family, especially if they have an expectation of financial provision, security and status. It is very hard for non-Christian families to understand how believers can reject the world and all its attractions, and place their trust in the Lord, willing to be of no reputation. If for example you have been educated privately at great expense in order to earn a good living, the decision to be a missionary can be misinterpreted as rejecting what the family has provided. It may be seen both as financial suicide and irresponsibility to society. Even Elisha went back to explain to his family that he was leaving to join Elijah in the ministry and say farewell to his parents (1 Kings 20). These pressures can prevent believers from moving out in faith to serve the Lord, which is why Jesus particularly mentions it (Matthew 10:37). We need to be single-minded about this major issue because it affects our lives so fundamentally, simply as a result of being in the world. We only have seventy years or so, and this short span determines not only where we spend eternity but also what treasure we have laid up in heaven. We need to understand the new kingdom we have chosen to live in.

'For the kingdom of God is not a matter of eating and drinking, but of righteousness, peace and joy in the Holy Spirit, because anyone who serves Christ in this way is pleasing to God and approved by men.' (Romans 14:17–18 NIV.)

We have been transferred out of the kingdom of darkness into the kingdom of God, and should have no desire to go back as the Israelites did after God freed them from Egypt. We cannot have it both ways because we cannot serve two masters. May it be clear from our lives which we have chosen to serve. Whichever master you serve will reward you at the end of the day and it will then seem futile to have laid up so much treasure on earth for someone else to use.

'Do not store up for yourselves treasures on earth, where moth and rust destroy, and where thieves break in and steal. But store up for yourselves treasures in heaven, where moth and rust do not destroy, and where thieves do not break in and steal. For where you treasure is, there your heart will be also.' (Matthew 6:19–21 NIV.)

This passage is half for the men and half for the women, because the moth destroys fabrics and rust eats steel. The treasure women have to beware of it clothes and fabrics such as carpets, curtains and linen, in other words the whole area of the home. If you long to be let loose in Libertys or Harrods with an open cheque book then you may have treasure in this area!

For the men it is usually cars. If you covet your neighbour's BMW or Porsche then the world has you striving for its treasure. In a matter of years that car will be on the scrapheap, whereas God is concerned with treasure that lasts for ever. In order not to be misunderstood here we need to consider Jesus who wore such an expensive garment woven in one piece that the soldiers at the cross did not want to divide it. The issue is not what you have, for you can have these things if you hold them lightly. The issue is where your heart is.

'The heart is deceitful above all things and beyond cure. Who can understand it?
"I the Lord search the heart and examine the mind, to reward a man according to his conduct, according to what his deeds deserve."'
(Jeremiah 17:9–10 NIV.)

The whole point is that our hearts deceive us. We may think we know our hearts but the Lord really knows. Often we do not realise how much evil still remains in our hearts even after conversion and sanctification, and God needs to circumcise them and change them from stone to flesh.

Many of the men God uses have had to give up everything for the sake of the kingdom. Nowadays it seems as if we have to give up nothing if an easy, comfortable gospel is preached with the organ playing softly in the background. Those who take up a cross are on their way to death. Jesus wants the old life crucified with Him and for us to be dead to the world. We have the opportunity to lay up treasure for eternity in heaven. To do that we need our hearts set on the things that are above (Colossians 3:2). So little is taught about heaven that there is an implied universalism, in other words that we are all equal and identical no matter what we do on the earth. This is not so as a Bible study on the crowns and rewards will show you. We all have the opportunity to invest our time, energy, dedication and love in the kingdom of God. May we all determine afresh that we will serve the Lord wholeheartedly and be constantly aware of the warning to which we are all vulnerable: 'See to it, brothers, that none of you has a sinful, unbelieving heart that turns away from the living God' (Hebrews 3:12 NIV.)

To conclude consider the words of Solomon whose heart led him astray: 'Above all else, *guard your heart*, for it is the wellspring of life.' (Proverbs 4:23 NIV.)

7

My sheep hear My voice

John 10:27

Having established that we are in the kingdom of God and there to serve Him, we need to know the king of that kingdom personally and nurture our relationship as a son of the king. God wants each of us to really know Him as a father. '. . . those who are led by the Spirit of God are sons of God. For you did not receive a spirit that makes you a slave again to fear, but you received the Spirit of sonship.' (Romans 8:14–15 NIV.)

As sons of God we are to be led by the Spirit of God. Each of us will give an account of how we have handled what God has entrusted to us, so it is important to be daily led by the Spirit as an *individual* son. The Holy Spirit wants to speak to *all* of us individually as God's sons. This is particularly important in the area of church leadership and counselling, as believers need to learn how to hear from God for themselves rather than expect someone else to do it for them. There is safety in a multitude of counsellors, but their role is to give confirmation and advice, not primary directional guidance. We need to listen for and recognise the voice of the Lord, and use the witness of the Spirit whether something is right or wrong. We also have the corrective promise if we go astray: 'Whether you turn to the right or to the left, your ears will hear a voice behind you saying "This is the way; walk in it."' (Isaiah 30:21 NIV.)

This is a crucial area for all those desiring to walk in the Spirit because hearing clearly from God is something we learn rather than something that just happens automatically and we risk making mistakes as part of that learning process. It is a still small voice, and to hear it we have to be still before God and give Him time to speak to us. Jesus would often spend all night praying to His Father, whereas we are sometimes more like the disciples and cannot last an hour without falling asleep. Inadequate prayer time and lack of discipline in this area is one of the commonest reasons why we don't hear clearly, and not God's lack of willingness to speak to us. We may subsequently plough on in the natural with our own thinking, assuming guidance to be sanctified common sense, and deny God the opportunity to speak clearly and directly on the matter.

We do have to make sure that our walk is not the natural walk of the senses, because they are simply not the same as God's.

'"For my thoughts are not your thoughts,
neither are your ways my ways," declares the Lord.
"As the heavens are higher than the earth,
so are my ways higher than your ways
and my thoughts than your thoughts."'

(Isaiah 55:8–9 NIV.)

This is actually saying that God does not think in the same way we do, nor does He act in the same way either. His way is the higher way, and that is the one we should be following. It is not the natural logical path of the mind. When Moses saw the burning bush he was told to take off

82

his shoes. They represented the natural walk, and we also have to take them off and put on the shoes of the Spirit, to walk in the Spirit and not the flesh. God wants His fellowship and communication with us to be as clear as when He called Samuel, whether in an audible voice or not. This happens in your prayer life and as you spend time with God. The disciples did not ask Jesus to teach them to heal the sick, cast out demons or raise the dead – they just got on and did it as instructed, but they did ask Jesus to teach them to pray, because they recognised that this was how He received His power and anointing from the Father. Both corporately and privately we need to learn to pray, including praying in the Spirit in tongues as described in Romans 8 and covered earlier.

'In the same way, the Spirit helps us in our weakness. We do not know what we ought to pray, but the Spirit himself intercedes for us with groans that words cannot express. And he who searches our hearts knows the mind of the Spirit, because the Spirit intercedes for the saints in accordance with God's will.' (Romans 8:26–27 NIV.)

The effect of this is not only to pray according to the mind of the Lord and achieve results in the heavens, but in a corporate situation praying in the Spirit will often lead to a prophecy, vision or word of knowledge for the situation that comes straight from heaven and is the key to the situation. The whole area of hearing from God is one that we should be comfortable with and not see as either extreme or unusual, but we do have to adjust to God's various ways of speaking to us. Let us therefore look at these different ways – dreams, visions and prophetic words.

'When a prophet of the Lord is among you,
I reveal myself to him *in visions*.
I speak to him *in dreams*.
But this is not true of my servant Moses;

he is faithful in all my house.
With him I speak face to face,
clearly and not in riddles;
he sees the form of the Lord.' (Numbers 12:6–8 NIV.)

Although this is an Old Testament reference, it illustrates God's chosen way of speaking by way of visions and dreams, and they are not always clear almost by design. The Lord contrasts Moses with whom He speaks clearly face to face with visions and dreams that are not clear and may be 'in riddles' that need interpreting.

Daniel could 'understand visions and dreams of all kind' and therefore interpreted Nebuchadnezzar's complex dream without even being told what it was. 'During the night the mystery was revealed to Daniel *in a vision.*' (Daniel 2:19 NIV.) There are many examples of God speaking to men in a dream or vision – Abraham, Jacob, Nebuchadnezzard, Pharoah's servants, Joseph, Solomon, etc., and in the New Testament too with Joseph, Peter, Paul, Pilate's wife etc.. Some are clear and obvious, for example Joseph being warned to flee to Egypt, while others seem quite meaningless at the time, such as Peter's vision of the sheet let down from heaven. He simply couldn't fathom it out!

We are currently seeing the fulfilment of the prophecy of Joel 2:28 quoted on the day of Pentecost:

'In the last days, God says,
I will pour out my Spirit on all people.
Your sons and daughters *will prophesy*,
Your young men *will see visions*,
Your old men *will dream dreams*.
Even on my servants, both men and women,
I will pour out my Spirit in those days,
and they will prophesy.' (Acts 2:17–18 NIV.)

Whether you are young and see visions or old and dream dreams you should be expecting God to speak to you in this way and indeed pray that He will. The reason He does it like this is because of the barrier of the natural mind and intellect, and it usually happens at night because your mind is asleep! God then speaks into your spirit, which then transfers it to your mind in the same way as receiving a prophecy. It is possible to dream in your natural mind, such as fantasies or past experiences and also for demonic dreams to be fed in unless you have put on the protective helmet of salvation, which you are supposed to sleep in! Christians should not have to put up with bad dreams if they pray the protection of the blood of Jesus before going to sleep, so even if you have had interrupted or disturbed sleep God can enable you to enjoy a good night's rest. Psalm 127:2 translated 'He giveth His beloved sleep' should read that He gives to His beloved *in* sleep, both rest and dreams. In some cases the dreams are prophetic in nature about the future, in others keys to situations almost like dreaming a word of wisdom rather than speaking it out. If there is no immediate interpretation the dreams should be stored up until God reveals the interpretation at the right time, as He is not a God of confusion but order.

Visions vary in length, clarity and purpose. For example in the same way that you imagine something in your mind, such as your living room at home, you receive a vision in your spirit. Sometimes it is a single picture, sometimes several one after the other and they will be clearer at different times. Even the border between thinking it is a dream and it actually happening can be very thin in a person's mind. When Peter was let out of prison in Acts 12 'he had no idea that what the angel was doing was really happening; *he thought he was seeing a vision.*' In other words a vision can be so real that you think it is actually happening or vice versa. Paul describes his vision: 'I must go on boasting. Although there is nothing to be gained, I will go on to *visions* and *revelations* from the Lord. I know a man in Christ who fourteen years ago was caught up to the third heaven. Whether it was in the body or out of the body I do not know – God knows. And I know that this man – whether in the body or apart from the body I do not know, but God knows – was caught up to Paradise. He heard inexpressible things, things that man is not permitted to tell.' (2 Corinthians 12:1–4 NIV.)

He was not sure whether he was physically there or not. Even the purpose of visions is not always clear, and we need to pray on each occasion for the correct meaning. Peter only realised what the vision about the sheet let down with unclean animals actually meant when Cornelius' servants appeared (Acts 10:19). Because this is a hard area for our minds to understand we do need to check visions both with Scripture and wise believers to avoid being misled. Many of the cults started off through someone having a 'vision' or 'angelic visitation', and the devil disguises himself as an angel of light in an attempt to deceive. That is why we have the witness of the Spirit and the biblical checks. If dreams and visions were not an important part of God's communication with us then there would be no point in attempting to counterfeit them. We do need to recognise that God speaks in this way and expect dreams and visions to be a normal part of our Christian experience, for we do all dream and can expect God to speak to us in this way if we ask Him.

'One night the Lord spoke to Paul in a vision: "Do not be afraid; keep on speaking, do not be silent. For I am with you, and no-one is going to attack and harm you, because I have many people in this city." So Paul stayed for a year and a half, teaching them the word of God.' (Acts 18:9 NIV.)

The promise of God is that 'My sheep hear my voice' and

we do need to be attuned to the Lord and the way He speaks. As well as in dreams and visions God will speak to us from Scripture and as we read a particular verse or passage the Holy Spirit will particularly underline it for us so that we know it is the word of the Lord for us. This is more than a general anointing on scripture as it is the specific witness of the Spirit for the appropriate verses that spring to life. God will often speak in this way and it should be a normal expectation.

The various ways that God speaks are not as direct as we would like if it was up to us. We would love to have Jesus appear in person and give perfect, explicit instructions to us individually. God however moves in the dimension of faith and expects us to invest our faith in the ways He has chosen. We do of course have the specific direct personal instructions from Jesus in the New Testament, which need to be treated as the direct word of the Lord, but we also have prophecy as one of the nine listed gifts of the Spirit. This can be given as a message for the Body of Christ in a meeting or as an individual personal prophecy. An example of a word for the Body of Christ is given to the church in Antioch: 'During this time some prophets came down from Jerusalem to Antioch. One of them, named Agabus, stood up and through the Spirit predicted that a severe famine would spread over the entire Roman world. (This happened during the reign of Claudius.) The disciples, each according to his ability, decided to provide help for the brothers living in Judea.' (Acts 11:27–29 NIV.)

The believers moved in faith and were therefore able to prepare for the famine. God is giving similar words today to churches to prepare for what is coming. Paul was given a personal prophecy just before going to Jerusalem: 'After we had been there a number of days, a prophet named Agabus came down from Judea. Coming over to us, he took Paul's belt, tied his own hands and feet with it and said, "The

Holy Spirit says, 'In this way the Jews of Jerusalem will bind the owner of the belt and will hand him over to the Gentiles.'"' (Acts 21:10–11 NIV.)

Although the disciples tried to persuade Paul to heed the warning he chose to go anyway, and the prophecy was of course fulfilled. Many Christians are receiving personal words from the Lord for the future, and need to be in faith about them even if they have not yet happened. The prophecy is there as an assurance that God will bring to pass anything He has promised and so that you can be in faith no matter what the visible circumstances might lead you to conclude.

God wants to speak to us in the same way that Jesus spoke constantly to the Father, and He is our example. We have not been abandoned to get on as best we can, but have the indwelling Holy Spirit, the Comforter who is alongside as our helper, and Jesus told the disciples that it was better that He should leave them so that the Holy Spirit could then come. May we not restrict or quench Him but allow Him to speak to us and lead us in the ways of the Lord.

8

Whatever is not of faith is Sin

Romans 14:23

The walk of the Spirit is a walk of faith because that is the
dimension in which God moves. If we are not walking in
faith towards God and His Word then as far as He is
concerned we are walking in unbelief, and that is sin.
Habakkuk 2:4 declares that 'the righteous shall live by his
faith'. We are also told that 'without faith it is impossible to
please God' (Hebrews 11:6). Faith is so fundamental to
moving on with God that we need to understand it and
learn to nurture it to the glory of God, who considers it to
be more precious than gold.

Faith is not something you either have or have not based
on whether God felt like giving it to you. This would be
both irrational and unfair. For that reason Paul is careful to
state that God has given to *each* person *the measure of faith*
(Romans 12:3). Clearly some people's measure has grown
more than others but no-one actually misses out on getting
their measure. It is like a seed that is planted at salvation.
We all have it but it needs to be fed and watered to allow it
to grow. Growth comes from hearing the Word of God
(Romans 10:17) and being tested and proved in greater and
greater areas. The more you know, understand, believe and
apply the Word of God, the more your faith will grow and
you will be able to reach out to God for more and more. For

example you start off moving in faith in small matters such as being in faith for your health and then as your faith grows you can pray for those not in health. Even that is by degrees of faith. You start off with the coughs and colds, aches and pains, and as you see these clearing up move on to harder cases. It is important always to stay within your faith and let God increase it by degrees. Occasionally you may receive the gift of faith referred to earlier which enables you to move beyond your measure of faith, but the point is that God gives you extra faith and you should not move into unbelief, because that shuts off the flow and anointing from heaven. When God asked Solomon what he wanted most he asked for wisdom. If I was asked the same question now the answer would definitely be *faith*, for it pleases God and allows the full manifestation of the Spirit of God. There is not enough faith exercised in the Body of Christ.

The biggest single obstacle to faith is unbelief about what the Bible says to be true. Whereas the world says 'Seeing is believing' God's way is the opposite – Believing is seeing. One of the paradoxes in the Christian life is that even if we have unbelief we still have faith, for the Holy Spirit inside us is always in perfect faith towards God's Word, whereas it is the natural mind that is in unbelief. In other words you can have both but unbelief blocks off the faith because it is sin and needs to be confessed and forgiven. Once you deal with the unbelief the faith is there according to the measure you have. The opposite of faith is not just unbelief but *sight* – in other words using the natural senses.

'We live *by faith, not by sight*' (2 Corinthians 5:7 NIV.)

This is a hard concept because most of us like to see where we are heading! If you want to walk purely in the natural realm you will never experience the walk of faith, because it is not visible to the natural eye. If you are a natural forward planner faith will be very hard for you as you have to unlearn the natural laws and learn the laws of the Spirit. Faith is of supreme value to God, who only moves in the faith area. He is permanently in faith about all His promises in the Bible, all the future, and everything He has prepared for His children. 'Now faith is being sure of what we hope for and certain of what we do not see. This is what the ancients were commended for.' (Hebrews 11:1 NIV.)

This verse summarises faith. The first part refers to the promises of God and His total faithfulness regarding all that He has promised us. Because He is all-knowing, all-powerful, eternal and cannot lie or change, we have total security in His word for our lives, whatever happens on the earth. That does not mean that everything is predestined but that God will make sure that every promise towards us will hold true. We need faith in God and His revealed word. If you are in unbelief about the Bible being the revealed Word of God you cannot walk in faith. Abraham trusted in God's word and was commended for his faith. Salvation is by faith. Healing is by faith. It is faith firmly grounded in the Bible.

'Being certain of what we do not see' or 'the evidence of things not seen' simply means not walking by sight in the natural realm but still believing God's Word to be certain, whether we actually see it come to pass or not. Abraham never received the geographical territory promised to him, and he is still in faith in heaven that Jesus will give it to his descendants precisely as promised when He returns to the earth to reign for one thousand years in the Millenial Kingdom. The promise was given to Abraham (Genesis 15:18) and God is committed to it. This is equally true of all the unfulfilled promises about Jesus. Any prophecy not fulfilled during Jesus' time on the earth will be literally fulfilled when He returns. We need to be in faith about this and believe it even though it may seem impossible. It certainly looks impossible that Israel will own Lebanon,

Syria, Iraq, Jordan, Saudi Arabia and part of Egypt in the foreseeable future, yet God has promised that it shall be so and we need to be in faith that it shall come to pass when Jesus returns. Much of Isaiah contains millenial prophecies based on Israel coming into the territorial promise and the Lord reigning personally in Jerusalem.

'In that day the Lord will thresh from the flowing Euphrates to the Wadi of Egypt, and you, O Israelites, will be gathered up one by one. And in that day a great trumpet will sound. Those who were perishing in Assyria and those who were exiled in Egypt will come and worship the Lord on the holy mountain in Jerusalem.' (Isaiah 27:12–13 NIV.)

We also need to be in faith about the Second Coming of Jesus to establish His Kingdom, and of course about the Rapture.

'But we know that when he appears, we shall be like him, for we shall see him as he is. Everyone who has this hope in him purifies himself, just as he is pure.' (1 John 3:2–3 NIV.)

This hope inside us is supposed to affect us. These are not just dry doctrines but part of the eternal purposes of God for us and we need to allow them to stir up our faith and encourage us to keep going.

Hebrews 11 is the key passage outlining those who lived by faith and it is too extensive to quote here. When you read it note the kinds of things they did by faith. Chapter 11 concludes: 'And what more shall I say? I do not have time to tell about Gideon, Barak, Samson, Jephthah, David, Samuel and the prophets, who through faith conquered kingdoms, administered justice, and gained what was promised; who shut the mouths of lions, quenched the fury of the flames, and escaped the edge of the sword; whose weakness was turned to strength; and who became powerful in battle and routed foreign armies. Women received back their dead, raised to life again. Others were tortured and refused to be released, so that they might gain a better resurrection. Some faced jeers and flogging, while still others were chained and put in prison. They were stoned; they were sawn in two; they were put to death by the sword. They went about in sheepskins and goatskins, destitute, persecuted and ill-treated – the world was not worthy of them. They wandered in deserts and mountains, and in caves and holes in the ground.

These were all commended for their faith, *yet none of them received what had been promised*.' (Hebrews 11:32–32 NIV.)

They were commended because they were in faith towards God despite all the circumstances and believed that God was still able to keep His word.

Faith will definitely be tested to the limit and proved to see how real it is. 'In this you greatly rejoice, though now for a little while you may have had to suffer grief in all kinds of trials. *These have come so that your faith* – of greater worth than gold, which perishes even though refined by fire – *may be proved genuine* and may result in praise, glory and honour when Jesus Christ is revealed.' (1 Peter 1:6–7 NIV.)

Testing is similar to attaching a rope to a branch to climb a tree. You test it by giving it a really strong tug with all your weight and then know it will support you while you climb. You are testing both the rope and the branch. The branch is like the Word of God and will support any weight. The rope is like faith and you need to be sure that you have a strong enough piece to be in faith for it to support you. It is the proving of your faith rather than a test you pass or fail, and once you have given the rope a good pull and proved it strong enough you then move out in faith and start to climb. Your faith is then proved genuine. Doubts, fears and unbelief will neutralise the faith we have, bringing us into the realm of natural sight, and even if we are in faith there can be so much unbelief in others that God is unable to act, as He will not move out of the dimension of faith. Jesus who was full of faith was hampered in Nazareth where he could do nothing because of *their* unbelief. That is why a prophet is not without honour except at home where he is known. If you are too well-known people see you in the natural, faith is suppressed and no-one believes you can do anything. Nothing therefore happens and that just confirms their suspicions! If it was true of Jesus it will be true of us, so the Holy Spirit is quenched and grieved.

It can even be the case that there is more unbelief in Christians than those who do not know the Lord, however strange that might seem. It can be easier for non-Christians to receive healing from God as a sign that He loves them and desires them to be saved, whereas believers can cut off the flow from God by being in unbelief and therefore miss the healing to which they are biblically entitled.

Unbelief comes from two main sources, which we need to examine. The first is the natural senses, in particular the natural mind.

'The man without the Spirit does not accept the things that come from the Spirit of God, for they are foolishness to him and he cannot understand them, because they are *spiritually discerned*. The spiritual man makes judgements about all things, but he himself is not subject to any man's judgement.' (1 Corinthians 2:14–15 NIV.)

The natural mind rejects faith as foolishness or presumption. It is illogical, unintellectual, irrational and dangerous. Now if we were dealing with 'faith healing' that would be true, since it is faith in faith, but we are dealing with faith in God who has made His will known and actually given us faith to use. We therefore trust in His eternal promises and His Word, which has substance and purpose. God has chosen the foolish things of this world including the poor and unintelligent to baffle the wise because He does not want natural wisdom to be involved in faith at all. We need to beware of the natural senses blocking faith.

Secondly there is the devil who is the father of lies and the accuser of the brethren. He knows how powerful faith is as he is the victim of faith in the areas of healing and deliverance and will therefore do his utmost to discredit Jesus, the Bible and Christians walking in faith. As God pours out the Holy Spirit on believers we can expect more attacks in these areas to shake our faith. Intellectual academics will produce 'evidence' that Jesus faked the miracles, never actually died but fainted, and the Bible was made up by early Christians to perpetuate the myth! Even some evangelical Christians now no longer accept the authority of scripture, despite the fact that Jesus quoted the Old Testament extensively, accepting all of it and having faith in all it said. The shield of faith is able to cope with all these arrows which just bounce off. Our faith will be attacked and tested with one of the main targets being the whole question of healing. The Bible declares that Jesus died for sickness as well as sin, as sickness was part of the curse on Adam from which we have been redeemed.

'He himself bore our *sins* in his body on the tree, so that we might die to sins and live for righteousness; by his wounds *you have been healed*' (1 Peter 2:24 NIV.)

'Surely he bore our griefs, and carried our sorrows: yet we did esteem him stricken, smitten of God and afflicted.

But he was wounded for our transgressions, he was chastised for our iniquities: the chastisement of our peace was upon him; and *with his stripes we are healed*.' (Isaiah 53:4–5 AV.)

Griefs which is translated infirmities in the NIV means sickness and pain (choli) and sorrows means pain (makob). If Jesus bore our sicknesses and pains and by His stripes we are healed, then this is a clear statement that Jesus died for sickness as well as sin, and healing is included in the

Atonement, if only we would believe it. There is still much unbelief in this area which quenches faith. Jesus spent much of His time healing the sick, told the disciples to do the same, and said that it would be part of the signs following believers that they too would heal the sick to illustrate that the gospel is true. The Holy Spirit gave the gift of healing to the Church to use actively and positively, and we should do so. There are biblical conditions for healing, and we need to fulfil these and be aware of them, but always be aware that healing is available from God as part of the New Covenant. May it never be true of us that Jesus can do nothing because of our unbelief.

In concluding on faith we need to have a positive confession that everything the Bible says about us is true whether we see the evidence or not. Faith does not need to see the visible evidence but believes because God says it. In Revelation the victory of the believer is described: 'They overcame him (Satan) by the blood of the Lamb and by the *word of their testimony*;' (Revelation 12:11 NIV).

What we confess out of our mouths is important and forms our testimony. It must be the word of faith that is able to overcome all satanic opposition. We can have faith to move mountains and need to speak it out of our mouths in every situation.

'I live by the faith of the Son of God' (Galatians 2:20 AV). Our high calling is the daily walk of faith.

9

He who loveth not his brother
1 John 4:20

Faith without works is dead (James 2:26). God has called us to good works that are the outworking of the faith we have. This practical area affects our lives and relationships both inside and outside the Body of Christ. It is self-evident that we must practise what we preach and keep all the commandments of Jesus, particularly the new commandment to love one another. Bad relationships cause tremendous problems and tension, and do need to be dealt with biblically and sorted out.

The starting point has to be us. No matter how much damage has been done to us in the past the key to our freedom is in our own hands and we need to move out in faith.

'We love because he first loved us. If anyone says, "I love God," yet hates his brother, he is a liar. For anyone who does not love his brother, whom he has seen, cannot love God, whom he has not seen. And he has given us this command: Whoever loves God must also love his brother.' (1 John 4:19–21 NIV.)

You sometimes hear it said that you don't need to like your brother as long as you love him! If you genuinely love him I cannot see how you can fail to like him because love is patient, kind, longsuffering and keeps no record of wrongs.

It seeks the best for the other person and a relationship will develop out of that. Even if he sins and is out of fellowship love will seek to help him back. Everyone has something likeable about them if we will see it and it is hard to believe that you are loved by someone who makes it clear they don't like you! Love must be genuine and a visible part of the fruit which the Holy Spirit is producing in our lives. This chapter seeks to remove those blockages to the free flow of love among the family of God.

One of the most common blockages is unforgiveness. It is amazing that Christians can refuse to forgive those who have wronged them after all that the Lord has forgiven them. The parable of the Unmerciful Steward in Matthew 18 was told in response to Peter's question – 'how many times shall I forgive my brother when he sins against me? Up to seven times?' We know that the answer is seventy times seven but the point is what happens to the one who will not forgive.

'In anger his master turned him over to the jailers until he should pay back all he owed. "This is how my heavenly Father will treat each of you unless you forgive your brother from your heart."' (Matthew 18:34–35 NIV.)

Immediately following Jesus' prayer in Matthew 6 He tells them: 'For if you forgive men when they sin against you, your heavenly father will also forgive you. But if you do not forgive men their sins, *your Father will not forgive your sins.*' (Matthew 6:14–15 NIV.)

This passage is not about salvation but relationship. Your salvation does not depend on forgiving your brother but on repentance and faith towards God. If however you subsequently will not forgive your brother you are out of fellowship with God because you have unconfessed and undealt with sin in your life and cannot experience God's forgiveness in this matter until you have dealt with it. It may be something that happened years ago, but even so you need to deal with it first of all in your own heart and then if the person concerned is aware of the situation by seeing them, phoning or writing according to what God tells you. If they are unaware it's best to leave it between you and God.

Alongside unforgiveness there is often resentment towards another. The other person may not have apologised or worse still thought there was nothing to apologise over! None of us should hold any resentment of any kind to anyone, as it grieves the Holy Spirit.

'And do not grieve the Holy Spirit of God, with whom you were sealed for the day of redemption. Get rid of all bitterness, rage and anger, brawling and slander, along with every form of malice. Be kind and compassionate to one another, forgiving each other, just as in Christ God forgave you.' (Ephesians 4:30–32 NIV.)

In the parable of the sower we are all described as soil, and we must keep ourselves weed-free, otherwise the Word of God will be choked and less fruitful. One weed to watch out for is the root of bitterness, which is very hard to get out if allowed to take root and draw sustenance from the soil. The Holy Spirit is able to make it shrivel up and die in the same way that Jesus cursed the fig tree, but it is better not to let it even take root.

'Make every effort to live in peace with all men and to be holy; without holiness no-one will see the Lord. See to it that no-one misses the grace of God and that *no bitter root grows up to cause trouble* and defile many.' (Hebrews 12:14–15 NIV.)

Rather we are to be rooted and grounded in love (Ephesians 3:17) and free from all these things affecting our lives. Unforgiveness, bitterness and resentment within the family, particularly between husband and wife, will do enormous damage and hinder the blessing of the Lord. If a husband mistreats his wife for example his prayers will be blocked and cut off. The word translated 'hindered' (ekkopto) means to be cut off: 'Husbands, in the same way be considerate as you live with your wives, and treat them with respect as the weaker partner and as heirs with you of the gracious gift of life, so that nothing will hinder your prayers.' (1 Peter 3:7 NIV.)

We are to bless one another and allow the Holy Spirit to pour out His love through us as we submit to the Word of God.

Parents and children need to forgive one another from the heart as mistakes are made in upbringing. We are either too strict or too lenient, too possessive or too unconcerned. It is one of those 'no win' situations with the problems the parents experienced often passed on to the children. We need to know the biblical principles of upbringing to ensure maximum happiness, peace and harmony and pre-empt rebellion at a later stage. The principle 'Train up a child in the way he should go and when he is old he will not turn from it' (Proverbs 22:6) works both ways and if you train him up badly it heaps up problems for later. Children reveal a lot about their parents!

If you have been damaged in any way in the past then there is healing through forgiveness by the power of the Spirit. Just as Jesus said 'Father, forgive them, they know not what they do' it is also true that much hurt is caused by ignorance and the sinful nature of man rather than deliberate evil intent, as it was in Jesus' case. Either way we need to forgive and allow the healing oil of the Spirit to heal the wound. Jesus came to bind up the broken hearted and release the prisoners (Isaiah 61:1), and we need to be open to let it happen so that relationships can be restored.

God wants purity and holiness in the Body of Christ and for us to have good relationships with one another, where we can be free to grow together and have our needs met. We owe it to each other and to the Lord.

'Finally, brothers, whatever is true, whatever is noble, whatever is right, whatever is pure, whatever is lovely, whatever is admirable – if anything is excellent or praiseworthy – think about such things.' (Philippians 4:8 NIV.) We should be occupied with Jesus and serving Him in the Body of Christ with our mind set on the things that are above. If only we thought about those things listed above, we would begin to live together in harmony and experience the blessing that God promises where there is unity and genuine love among the believers.

'Behold, how good and pleasant it is for brethren to dwell together in unity! It is like the precious ointment upon the head, that runs down upon the beard, even Aaron's beard: that went down to the skirts of his garments; As the dew of Hermon, and as the dew that descended upon the mountains of Zion: for there the Lord commanded the blessing, even life for evermore.' (Psalm 133 AV.)

10

Fan into flame the gift of God

2 Timothy 1:6

Having seen some of the ways that we can suppress or quench the fire of the Holy Spirit we now need to look at how to positively develop our walk with God and be fully equipped for the ministry to which He has called us. This means learning to live by the laws and principles of the Kingdom of God, and to invest our faith that God who has begun a good work in each of us will bring it through to completion. The flesh, the natural man and the Spirit are opposed to one another, and we have to put off the old and put on the new in order to be able to walk in the Spirit.

'For the kingdom of God is not a matter of eating and drinking, but of righteousness, peace and joy in the Holy Spirit' (Romans 14:17 NIV).

'For God did not give us a spirit of timidity, but a spirit of power, of love and of self-discipline.' (2 Timothy 1:7 NIV.)

These two passages highlight six aspects of the Spirit led life that God has called us to and we should expect them in increasing measure.

Jesus tells us to hunger and thirst after righteousness because we shall be filled. Although we have the imputed righteousness of Jesus, Paul is really writing here about living out our part, in other words right living. We are to live by God's standards and be blameless, innocent and holy. This will affect all the areas of our lives. It means submitting rigidly to all the laws of the land, including speed restrictions and yellow lines, being 100% honest about our tax return, submitting to our employer and being a good employee, and being willing to submit to the leadership of our church. God wants us to do these things for Him, as unto the Lord because they are the environment within which He is training us in sonship. If Jesus had to learn obedience (Hebrews 5:8) then we have to as well, and co-operate with the Holy Spirit to produce the peaceable fruit of righteousness (Hebrews 12:11).

God has also called us to peace. The kingdom of God is not in turmoil and confusion. It is peaceful and orderly and God wants us to be peaceful and orderly too. Jesus left us His peace which the world cannot give (John 14:27). It is part of His kingdom and we should constantly experience the peace of the Lord. In order to do that we need a right relationship with God, our family and other believers. This means constantly walking in fellowship with God as Jesus did, being in unity and harmony with our family, and being able to fellowship freely with everyone, as there are no personality clashes or friction. If any of these areas is not right we cannot enjoy the peace that God intends for us. The Bible is very practical and tells us how to deal with each of these situations. As far as God is concerned we may need to confess our sin or get back into faith on some issue. With the family it may be getting the roles right so that the husband can lead by example, treating his wife correctly and making sure that the children are obedient. Problems with other believers may just need an apology and a willingness to forgive and forget. The key to not quenching the Spirit is to make sure that you are walking in peace and if something comes up to deal with it that day and not let the sun go down on your anger. The longer you leave it, the harder it is and it goes on affecting you. If you are not in peace ascertain why and allow the Spirit to show you the corrective steps to get back into peace.

The kingdom of God is meant to be full of joy and the happiest place to be. The Holy Spirit is full of joy and we need to be less British and reserved about the joy we have inside. If anyone could ever accuse us of being miserable then we are quenching the Spirit who very definitely is not! This needs to be expressed in our praise and worship as well as our homes and we should be known as the happiest people around. This is not just a good testimony for others but allows the Holy Spirit to express through us how He feels no matter where we are. When Stephen was stoned and his face glowed, it was surely with the joy of the Lord as he saw Jesus, and the joy of the Lord was his strength. It enabled him to be in victory during his stoning and he just 'fell asleep' and passed into heaven (Acts 7:55–60).

God has not given us a spirit of fear but of power. Fear is able to quench the Spirit because it effectively paralyses a believer and intimidates him. This can be true not only in meetings but individually and we need to experience the perfect love of Jesus that casts out fear. If you have fear then it is not from God and you need to be freed from it (Psalm 34:4). God has given us power and we need to be sure that we are not limiting this power and quenching the Spirit. God has given us power to be witnesses and to have authority over all the principalities and powers that seek to oppose and hinder the work of God. We are in a spiritual fight whether we like it or not, and we are targets. We need to move in the power of God and learn what power we have. We can pull down spiritual strongholds, pray obstacles out of the way, cast out demons in the name of Jesus and move in the gifts of the Spirit. We are positionally seated with Christ, higher than the angels, the fallen angels, unredeemed man, the animals and the plants. We need to see it and realise what God has entrusted to us. It requires a revelation of the Holy Spirit.

'I keep asking that the God of our Lord Jesus Christ, the glorious Father, may give you the *spirit of wisdom and revelation*, so that you may know him better. I pray also that the eyes of your heart may be enlightened in order that you may *know* the hope to which he has called you, the riches of his glorious inheritance in the saints, and his *incomparably great power for us who believe*. That power is like the working of his mighty strength, which he exerted in Christ when he raised him from the dead and seated him at his right hand in the heavenly realms, far above all rule and authority, power and dominion, and every title that can be given, not only in the present age, but also in the one to come. And God placed all things under his feet and apointed him to be head over everything *for the church*, which is his body, the fullness of him who fills everything in every way.' (Ephesians 1:17–23 NIV.)

Once we see it we can then move in faith and prove it to be true in our own experience. God does not want us holding back with what He has chosen to give us. Along with the power we have love, which is the very nature of God, for power without love is dangerous. May we allow God always to motivate us with the love of the Father, and to let His perfect love remove any fear we could otherwise have.

God has also given us a sound mind or self-discipline. We have it now and need to allow God the order that comes from discipline. In other words it should be clear that the Holy Spirit has produced an ordered, stable and mature life out of whatever muddles there were when we were saved. This is then a credit to the work of the Spirit and shows that we have come under new management. It is important not to fight it while it is happening! Part of that new self-discipline will be time to pray, time to study the Bible, time with the family and time with other believers all in a proper balance.

If we really want to be on fire for God we have to function as fire does. It is not an emotive issue based on standing up at a service or meeting on dedication. It is like the song about love – don't talk of love *show me!*

We can now consider seven marks of being on fire for God and see how well we measure up to them, because where the Spirit is unquenched these marks should be in evidence.

First of all fire gives off warmth. When we are on fire for God the effect should be that we warm others around us, just like sitting round a warm fire. Sometimes we use the phrase that we warm to someone. It is meant to be like that when the Holy Spirit controls our personalities, as He never was and will never become a cold person. In other words there should be a warming effect by being with someone burning for God. This happened on the road to Emmaus when two disciples walked with Jesus.

'Were not our hearts burning within us while he talked with us on the road and opened up the Scriptures to us?' (Luke 24:32 NIV.)

Whatever personality we may naturally have the Holy Spirit can change us to be more like Jesus so that others warm to us and see that the Lord is a warm person.

Fire gives off light. The darker it is the more visible the light even from a great distance. God wants us to be salt and light for Him, so that others will clearly see. To do this we have to be burning our oil.

'*You* are the light of the world. A city on a hill cannot be hidden. Neither do people light a lamp and put it under a bowl. Instead they put it on its stand, and it gives light to everyone in the house. In the same way, *let your light* shine before men, that they may see your good deeds and praise your Father in heaven' (Matthew 5:13–16 NIV).

God desires a witness for Himself on the earth for those not saved and the light we have is meant to point them to the Lord. This implies that it has to be something supernatural otherwise they would not praise God for it, but assume it was part of our natural character. The passage implies that in our role as ambassadors and witnesses for Jesus there will be supernatural signs following. Jesus wants us to make clearly visible what we have and not to hide it. If we are on fire for God there will be signs following our ministry, because God Himself does not want the gospel to be hidden. Even if men prefer darkness to light (John 3:19) God wants that light for those who will look to it. John describes Jesus as the light of the world (John 1:9) and that ministry has been extended to us, so that we fully represent Him.

Fire is used in cooking and to prepare food. The Bible describes itself as milk (1 Peter 2:2) and meat (1 Corinthians 3:2) and the ministry of a teacher is to prepare and present that food so that the believers are nourished and fed. A man on fire for God will not serve up spiritual food reheated from cold, but garnish the meat in such a way that it makes the listener come back for more. It may mean turning the meat into mince so that it can be digested more easily and spending hours in preparation. If you want to be on fire for God then you should ask God to teach you how to prepare spiritual food for the Body of Christ, and seek to develop the ministry of feeding the flock. Too much is left to the 'Bible teachers' when this should be a feature of Christians going on with God, that they both know the Word and can teach it.

'In fact, though by this time *you ought to be teachers*, you need someone to teach you the elementary truths of God's word all over again. You need milk, not solid food! Anyone who lives on milk, being still an infant, is not acquainted with the teaching about righteousness. But solid food is for the mature, who by constant use have trained themselves to distinguish good from evil.' (Hebrews 5:12–14 NIV.)

Fire is used for purifying. This is a ministry needed in the Body of Christ so that it is pure and it takes a man on fire for God to do it. God is described in Malachi: 'He will sit as a refiner and purifier of silver; he will purify the Levites and refine them like gold and silver' (Malachi 3:2 NIV).

The principle is to heat up the substance so that the impurities come to the surface where they are then skimmed off. In terms of ministry a man on fire for God can do that because the warmth of his presence enables those with deep problems to allow themselves to be affected by the warmth which brings up the impurities which are then dealt with and removed. In other words those on fire for God can have a counselling type of ministry from the Holy Spirit that purifies the Body of Christ and prepares the Bride of Christ for Jesus. This can also be done through the anointed word of prophecy or knowledge so that the word is received and results in the Body being purified.

Fire is also used for melting or welding. If you are on fire for God your heat can affect believers who come near you so that some of the heat is transferred. You can melt those iced-up for some reason or other, and restore life to the frozen parts. This is partly how the Body of Christ will be formed into one. God wants to weld us together as a single unit but with many parts, and it will take the fire of the Holy Spirit and men who will be used by God to do this. Unity will not come because everyone decides to forget their differences, but will be a work of the Spirit uniting us in a bond.

Fire is used for protection. God is concerned to protect the weak and defenceless in the Body of Christ and it is the role of the man on fire for God to act in a protective capacity. This means being aware of those most vulnerable and making sure that they are safe and living in peace and stability. In one sense it is a passive role and expresses a zeal and concern for the whole house of God.

Lastly fire is used for destruction. It is the element that God has chosen for the final destruction of the devil in the lake of fire, and God uses it in many other places in a similar way. The earth will be destroyed with fire at the end of the Millenium. As far as the man of God is concerned we need the fire of the Holy Spirit to destroy the works of the devil and give him a foretaste of the lake of fire. If we are on fire for God then we should be seeing the devil's work destroyed in the name of Jesus. Elijah did this both with the prophets of Baal and also the two groups of fifty men sent to capture him. In Indonesia there have been recent examples of God acting in a similar way and burning up idols. The point is that it is part of God's ministry for us to have dominion over demonic principalities and powers and to destroy the work they are doing, whether with literal fire or not. A man on fire for God will see God move in this way so that the authority we have in the heavens is established here on the earth.

When the disciples were baptised in the Holy Spirit tongues of fire rested on each one of them. They then all spoke in tongues. There is a link here because tongues are part of the anointing that comes on you when you are filled with the Spirit. In other words part of being on fire for God is the ministry of tongues as a spiritual weapon in prayer and ministry.

It is quite likely that not all the aspects of being on fire for God are functioning in their fullness in our lives, because there is a natural tendency in all of us to hold back and be cautious or conservative. This may be a national habit because it does not happen in some other countries where God is really allowed to move in power, and as a result the people there see more visible evidence of the power of God. The question then follows what should we do if we are quenching the Holy Spirit and not seeing those things that the Bible implies are normal but we consider exceptional?

We need to realise that God has lit a fire in each of us at salvation and however dimly it is burning it hasn't actually gone out.

'A bruised reed he will not break, and a smouldering wick he will not snuff out'. (Matthew 12:20 NIV.)

When Paul writes to Timothy he reminds him that he has a flame and it isn't burning as it should. Paul had prayed for him earlier and he had received a ministry, probably through a word of a prophecy, which had not yet come to pass.

'I remind you to fan into flame the gift of God, which is in you through the laying on of my hands' (2 Timothy 1:6 NIV).

It was there but latent. That can be the case with many of us. We may have had a word from the Lord about our ministry and that initial fire of enthusiasm has died down. Now is the time to start to fan that little flame and seek to be on fire with the ministry God has given you. Ask the Lord to refresh you with a new vision of that calling and press on into it. May we not be smouldering wicks that were once alight but brightly burning torches for the Lord as he makes His ministers to be flames of fire (Psalm 104:4).

Part III

The Walk of the Spirit

Introduction

The power of the Holy Spirit is described as 'dunamis' from which we get the word dynamite. It is a measure of the power that is within us that God wants released into effective use for Him. We need to encourage this flame that God has lit in each one of us to flare up to enable us to be on fire and function in the way fire does. Often we see others apparently moving ahead and God doing mighty things in their lives, whereas we may be comparatively static. It can almost seem arbitrary, as if God has especially chosen to reveal Himself to them for some unknown reason. This is not usually the case at all for there is a reason!

'"So I say to you: *ask* and it will be given to you; *seek* and you will find; *knock* and the door will be opened to you. For *everyone* who asks receives; he who seeks finds; and to him who knocks, the door will be opened."' (Luke 11:9–10 NIV.)

The whole purpose of the parable from which this is taken is that we have to stick at it, be persistent and in fact make a nuisance of ourselves until we get what we need. We need to ask, to seek, and to knock. That implies that we know what to ask for, what to seek after and what door we want opened. These are three keys Jesus tells us to use.

111

In this section we shall look at three key principles in the life of the Spirit which are all things that *we* do: firstly prayer, second praise and thirdly moving in faith. We shall also look at the fruit of the Spirit as a sign of maturity in the believer, and finally at how we can imitate the early Church.

11

You do not have because you do not ask God

James 4:2

We all know how important prayer is without it needing to
be restated. However we do not always achieve through it
all that God wants and it is one of those paradoxes about
His nature that He chooses to work through our prayers
and not independently, which He could of course do. We
therefore need to be sure that our praying is not limited to
what we want but what He wants us to pray.

As far as our own lives are concerned Jesus has given us
one of the most open-ended promises possible, namely that
God will give us *anything* we ask for in His name. If we
therefore do not have anything it is either because we have
not asked for it, or if we have asked, it has been incorrectly.

'You do not have, because you do not ask God. When
you ask, you do not receive, because you ask with wrong
motives, that you may spend what you get on your
pleasures.' (James 4:2–3 NIV.)

The principle is that if we ask with the right motives
in the name of Jesus we shall receive. If we do not receive
this is the place to seek the reason. The promise of Jesus
opens up tremendous possibilities for the active prayer.
'"If you remain in me and my words remain in you, ask
whatever you wish, and it will be given you. This is to my
Father's glory, that you bear much fruit, showing

yourselves to be my disciples"' (John 15:7–8 NIV).

If we remain connected to the vine, in fellowship and obedient to Jesus' commands then He will give us whatever we ask for, which is up to *us*. The reason for this is so that we can reveal the blessing of God on our lives as a sign to the world, not to feed our self-indulgences. The phrase 'in my name' has been misunderstood and used too loosely, tagged onto the end of prayers in the hope that this will ensure a positive answer! We need to understand all that God requires of us to be able to receive in the way Jesus intends.

'If any of you lacks wisdom, he should ask God, who gives generously to all without finding fault; and it will be given to him. But when he asks, he must *believe* and *not doubt*, because he who doubts is like a wave of the sea, blown and tossed by the wind. That man should not think he will receive anything from the Lord; he is a *doubleminded* man, unstable in all he does.' (James 1:5–8 NIV.)

This little passage can often be the reason for unanswered prayer, because it highlights the issue of faith. We have to be singleminded, sure of what we want, sure it's biblically correct and good and proper for us to receive for our Christian walk and ministry. Only if all these are true can we ask in faith in the name of Jesus and believe for it to happen.

It is important that we learn to pray to the *Father* in the name of Jesus. This may sound odd but many people pray to Jesus or the Father or even a mixture of the two in the same prayer! Jesus is quite specific about this and does not tell us to ask Him and He'll then ask the Father for us. He tells us to ask *direct* in His name, because He has secured this access for *us*. This is the way the Trinity operates. The Holy Spirit inside us prompts us to pray to the Father in the name of Jesus. Prayer is a privilege and a wonderful gift we can use. We can actually influence God because He wants us to be involved in what is happening on the earth and prayers do influence Him. An excellent example of this is in the Old Testament.

'In those days Hezekiah became ill and was at the point of death. The prophet Isaiah son of Amoz went to him and said, "This is what the Lord says: Put your house in order, because you will die; you will not recover."

Hezekiah turned his face to the wall and prayed to the Lord, "Remember, O Lord, how I have walked before you faithfully and with wholehearted devotion and have done what is good in your eyes." And Hezekiah wept bitterly.

Before Isaiah had left the middle court, the word of the Lord came to him: "Go back and tell Hezekiah, the leader of my people, 'This is what the Lord, the God of your father David, says: I have heard your prayer and seen your tears; I will heal you. On the third day from now you will go up to the temple of the Lord. I will add fifteen years to your life. And I will deliver you and this city from the hand of the king of Assyria.'"' (2 Kings 20:1–6 NIV.)

In fact to confirm the word of the Lord God made the shadow go back ten steps. If God was willing to do that for Hezekiah because he humbled himself He is no less willing to do it for His children today. Where there is repentance and humility God will move in love and grace for the sick person, maybe even adding extra years that would otherwise be lost.

The situation we have in the New Testament is better than that in the Old Testament because answered prayer is no longer by grace alone but also by invitation. God acted out of grace to Hezekiah; we have grace plus the invitation to ask. This is not based on merit because we have earned enough favour and goodwill to ask with a reasonable chance of success but boldness to ask in the name of Jesus believing the Word of God. This is an important principle because we tend to be reluctant to ask God for the big things we need because we doubt His grace and love towards us. The result is underasking and an absence of the visible provision of God. It is better to overask if anything, but even that is not possible because we are told to pray about everything, not just the things we feel we need. There is nothing like a crisis to get Christians praying about things that maybe could have been avoided if they had prayed sooner. We need to see that God's plans for us are for good. '"For I know the plans I have for you," declares the Lord, "plans to prosper you and not to harm you, plans to give you a hope and a future. Then you will call upon me and come and pray to me, and *I will listen to you*. You will seek me and find me when you seek me with all your heart . . ."' (Jeremiah 29:11–13 NIV.)

We need to know that God wants the best for us and always hears our prayers. When Jesus prayed for Lazarus He reaffirmed this: 'Then Jesus looked up and said, "Father, I thank you that you have heard me. I knew that *you always hear me*, but I said this for the benefit of the people standing here, that they may believe that you sent me."' (John 11:41–42 NIV.)

We need to know that our prayers are heard and answered, either yes, no, later, wait or whatever. The assumption must not be that the answer is always yes! If we really do know and understand that God always answers this should stir up our faith to pray much more fervently about those things that really are important. There is an area of confusion about the two different types of prayer and what praying in the name of Jesus is meant to achieve. Although all prayer is in His name, because that is the way we have access to God, it does nevertheless differ in purpose and faith. There is the normal straight asking type of prayer which is quite valid. For example we expect God to guide us, so we commit our way to Him and pray about decisions until we have peace and the witness of the Spirit.

We ask for things wanting one answer but willing to accept another. The answer is not automatically 'yes' because you pray in the name of Jesus! Even Jesus prayed for release from the cup of suffering (Matthew 26:39) but of course prayed that the Father's will should be done. We too can pray for what we would prefer to happen but always in the context of the Father's will. That is precisely why we need to know and understand His will in those areas where He has specifically revealed it. This leads on to the second type of prayer which James describes where we know what we should be praying for and God wants the specific directed prayer of faith to release His provision. This type of prayer is much more purposeful and directed because we know what we want and stick at it in prayer until we see the results. This requires singlemindedness and stickability and we do need to know that we are praying for something to which we are biblically entitled.

Let us look at the example of John's letter: 'Beloved, I wish above all things that thou mayest prosper and be in health, even as thy soul prospereth.' (3 John 2 AV.)

This highlights two major areas we need to be in faith and praying about – prosperity and health. We need to know the mind of the Lord on both. Prosperity means the abundant provision of God in every area so that you have enough food, warmth, clothing and a home. Jesus lived in prosperity as far as the Bible is concerned and although He didn't have a home stayed regularly with Martha and Mary in Bethany. Prosperity is not riches or a high standard of living despite popular teaching that this is a sign of God's approval. Proverbs gives the balance:

'Give me neither poverty nor riches,
but give me only my daily bread.
Otherwise I may have too much and disown you
and say, 'Who is the Lord?'

> Or I may become poor and steal,
> and so dishonour the name of my God.'
>   (Proverbs 30:8–9 NIV.)

In these days where materialism has spilled over into the church we need to be praying that God will not give us riches that compete with Him for our time and affection. Solomon found this to his cost and the prosperity he had led him into sin. Ecclesiastes is the book of his regrets for missed opportunities. If only Christians would see this then a lot less time would be wasted asking God for wealth, which is what it boils down to. It is up to God to determine our standard of living and we need to learn to be content with what we have. The other area is of course health and again we need to know how to pray correctly both when we enjoy health and when we are one degree under. Many Christians are missing out on health by believing that it is somehow God's will for them to be sick and therefore accepting it passively. Healing is included in the Atonement as we have seen and we can therefore move in faith in this area until we see our physical bodies living in health.

The James 1 type of prayer is appropriate for both financial and physical blessing and we need to be single-minded about both and invest our faith for God's provision. In David's day there was no unemployment benefit, no social security and no National Health Service. Life was a great deal tougher than now yet David could still write:

> 'I was young and now I am old,
> yet *I have never seen the righteous forsaken*
> or their children begging bread.' (Psalm 37:25 NIV.)

Elijah was fed by the ravens when all other natural supply ran out. We need to pray in God's daily provision and never take it for granted, because one day there may be famine in the land as part of the birth-pangs of the Tribulation. Health is a difficult area because of the Fall and all creation is subject to decay and death, nevertheless we should press on into increasing health and pray actively when we are sick expecting God to restore us to health. It is worth just mentioning that sickness can be both physical and spiritual in origin and if God shows you that the cause is spiritual then pray against the sickness or spirit of infirmity in the name of Jesus, which is the only effective remedy. You can have a medical cure for a medical sickness, i.e. pill A will cure sickness A, but you cannot have a medical cure for a spiritual sickness; you need a spiritual cure that only God can give. Either way you should look to the One risen with healing in His wings.

We need to experience more of the prayer of faith where we hear from God and move out in faith or invest our faith singlemindedly to achieve some goal or objective. We need to know what to pray for and stick at it until it happens. Some things seem to take a long time but there can be spiritual reasons blocking the answer. We are given a glimpse of this in Daniel. Three times a day Daniel would pray. Several occasions are recorded where Daniel had a visitation from Gabriel or another angel. On one of these occasions the angel said: ('Then he continued), "Do not be afraid, Daniel. Since the first day that you set your mind to gain understanding and to humble yourself before your God, your words were heard, and I have come in response to them. But the prince of the Persian kingdom resisted me twenty one days."' (Daniel 10:12–13 NIV.)

We are not dealing with flesh and blood, but principalities and powers and they have power over nations, cities and individuals which have to be prayed against to clear the spiritual atmosphere for the work of God. This is something God reveals so that we can pray spiritual rulership over specific areas because we have been given authority to do so. Satan actually has a headquarters on the earth. When Jesus writes to the church in Pergamum He says 'I know where you live – where Satan has his throne' (Revelation 2:12). In other words Satan was based in Pergamum. Some think he is now based on the West Coast of the USA possibly San Francisco, which is the world homosexual capital and full of every imaginable cult. Wherever it is the point is that there is a hierarchy of demonic principalities and powers and the Christians need to be praying against it and exercising spiritual rulership. This is a corporate responsibility for the earth, but locally where you live it is up to the local believers who should be spiritually aware what is happening. If we are to grow in knowledge and wisdom in prayer we need to see that the issues are spiritual in essence and take up the burden to pray. God wants us to achieve rulership through prayer and negligence in this area limits what is done for the kingdom. The battle is in the heavens even though the manifestation of the result is seen on the earth.

It is because of spiritual warfare that we are given the ability to pray in the Spirit and in tongues, because the devil does not understand them. It is a bit like praying to God in code as He does understand them and then the power of God is released. We have tremendous power and spiritual authority in the name of Jesus and as we pray against principalities and powers we shall see situations turned on their heads. We are not supposed to be on the defensive and have been intimidated into a defeatist attitude through failing to realise who and what we are in Jesus. We are supposed to be *more* than conquerors (Romans 8:37). Most of us would settle for just being a conqueror! The defeatist attitude has even crept in to the way a passage is translated: 'When the enemy shall come in like a flood, the Spirit of the Lord shall lift up a standard against him.' (Isaiah 59:19 AV.)

120

This of course implies that Satan comes in like a flood drowning everything. A flood is the uncontrollable overflow of water that pushes everything out of the way. This is not true of the devil. He is not like a flood and definitely containable. It is the Holy Spirit who is like a flood—rivers of living water. The point is that there is no comma after flood. It should therefore read: When the enemy comes in *like a flood the Spirit of the Lord shall lift up a standard against him.* The devil comes in and faces this mountain of water against him that he cannot resist and is swept away. The whole meaning of the passage changes and our attitude should too. We must not expect him to come flooding in uncontrollably, but rather expect him to be flooded out by the Spirit of the Lord. If you can see this then your attitude to prayer will change from being defensive to offensive. The devil is meant to be defending his territory from the advancing army of God not vice versa! That is true individually for each one of us, in our churches and in the nation. It's not a factor of numbers but power from above. Down through history men have changed the destinies of nations through prayer. Britain could have been occupied in 1940, liberated by the Russians and now be a communist state but the nation prayed. Historians have never understood why we weren't invaded. We have the responsibility for the spiritual state of the nation as God has given us this power in prayer. Our future depends on it.

On a global front Israel is the key to God's prophetic timetable and we are told to pray for the peace of Jerusalem:

'Pray for the peace of Jerusalem: they shall prosper that love thee.
Peace be within thy walls, and prosperity within thy palaces.

For my brethren and companions' sakes, I will now say,
Peace be within thee.
Because of the house of the Lord our God I will seek thy
good.' (Psalm 122:6–9 AV.)

If we are to grow in the walk of the Spirit God is going to call on us to be more involved with His purposes on the earth and we are going to be prompted to pray some unusual prayers. We are now seeing the spirit of militant Islam released over the earth and we need to raise up the standard of the Spirit. Indeed the Christians in Jerusalem believe that it was only the prayers of the interceding believers that held off an invasion from the north in 1983. God will not permit Israel to be destroyed but our prayers count. Although there is an overall prophetic timetable that does not mean it is pre-determined and even the time of the Rapture is affected by our prayers. We need that revelation of the great purposes of God and to know how much He looks to us to pray. This chapter is meant to give you a greater revelation of the amazing power of prayer that has been entrusted to us. It is much greater than is generally realised, otherwise the prayer meetings in the churches would be packed. If we want to move on with God then we have to be men and women of prayer knowing how to pray both with our minds and in the Spirit, for ourselves and our nation, for the work and kingdom of God to be established on the earth. There is no limit to what can be achieved if we will use what God has given us.

'They devoted themselves to the apostles' teaching and to the fellowship, to the breaking of bread and *to prayer*. Everyone was filled with awe, and many wonders and miraculous signs were done by the apostles.' (Acts 2:42–43 NIV.)

12

The Lord inhabits the praises of His People

Psalm 22:3

God has the right to praise as His due, firstly for who He is, the creator of the universe and all in it and secondly for all that He has done for us in making provision for our eternal salvation and our life here on the earth. It is one of the basic biblical requirements of believers to praise the Lord God of Heaven. In order to do this meaningfully we need a revelation of God as our Heavenly Father and that He is the God of love.

When God created the earth His provision was perfect. There was abundant food, the climate was perfect, the animals and plants thrived and Adam and Eve walked in fellowship with God. God saw that it was good. Even though we now see fallen creation it is still quite marvellous and reveals the God who is worthy to be praised for all the variety and detail of the plants and creatures. Indeed creation is where God has revealed Himself to every person. 'For since the creation of the world God's invisible qualities – his eternal power and divine nature – have been clearly seen, being understood from what has ben made, so that *men are without any excuse.* For although *they knew God,* they neither glorified him as God nor gave thanks to him' (Romans 1:20–21 NIV).

This passage states that every person is born with an

awareness of God through creation and therefore rejection of God is a deliberate choice. God expects us to glorify Him and give Him thanks. Praise is an acknowledgement that God is God and He is worthy to be praised. Humanism, atheism and evolution deny God the praise that is rightfully His, for we are fearfully and wonderfully made. If we are believers then God expects praise from us as part of the daily walk and relationship and not just in meetings or services. It is part of the walk of the Spirit.

Not only can we praise God for who He is but also for what He has done. Our salvation alone is quite priceless, apart from all the other blessings God gives to those who love Him. Deuteronomy 28 lists the blessings which Old Testament believers were entitled but we have been blessed in Christ with *every* spiritual blessing (Ephesians 1:3).

'Praise the *Lord*, O my soul;
all my inmost being, praise his holy name,
Praise the *Lord*, O my soul,
and *forget not all his benefits*.
He *forgives* all my sins
and *heals* all my diseases;
he *redeems* my life from the pit
and *crowns* me with love and compassion.
He *satisfies* my desires with good things,
so that my youth is renewed like the eagle's'
(Psalm 103:1–5 NIV.)

We need to be aware how important praise is in the move of the Spirit and why there is so much emphasis on it. God delights in being exalted to His rightful position in our lives and responds to those who do this. When we acknowledge the lordship of Jesus it releases power towards us because God wants to work in our lives and as we decrease so He increases the measure of power He pours out. In other words if we do things His way then we will definitely see success because God never fails. The principle of praise first is illustrated in the way God organised the army to capture Jericho. The seven priests with their seven trumpets went out first in front of the ark, which is where God was. We might have thought we'd have God first, then the trumpets, then the army, but the principle was *praise first* with God following the praise. It is as if praise prepared the way of the Lord. God wanted the people to see that He gave the victory and praise was an aknowledgement of this. Another illustration is when Jehoshaphat fought Ammon and Moab: '"Listen, King Jehoshaphat and all who live in Judah and Jerusalem! This is what the *Lord* says to you: 'Do not be afraid or discouraged because of this vast army. For *the battle is not yours but God's.*'"' (2 Chronicles 20:15). They are then told to take up their positions, stand firm and see the deliverance of God.

'As they set out, Jehoshaphat stood and said, "Listen to me, Judah and people of Jerusalem! Have faith in the *Lord* your God and you will be upheld; have faith in his prophets and you will be successful." After consulting the people, Jehoshaphat appointed men to sing to the *Lord*, and to *praise him for the splendour of his holiness* as they went out at the head of the army, saying:

"Give thanks to the *Lord*,
for his love endures for ever."

As they began to sing and praise, the *Lord* set ambushes against the men of Ammon and Moab and Mount Seir who were invading Judah, and they were defeated.' (2 Chronicles 20:20–22 NIV.)

They acknowledged that the battle was God's, but nevertheless took up their positions. We too need to see that many of the battles we fight could be won by praise if we would only see that the battle was His.

David knew about praise and arranged for four thousand Levites to praise the Lord in the new temple Solomon was to build (1 Chronicles 23:5). They were to stand every morning to thank and praise the Lord, to do so again in the evening and again whenever burnt offerings were presented on Sabbaths and Feast Days (1 Chronicles 23:30–31). It was a ministry in itself. Having seen the priesthood of all believers we now take on this duty, and it is no longer the role of the appointed priests but ours.

In the move of the Spirit praise should be a spontaneous outpouring from those filled with the Spirit. This is one reason why you need free and open meetings because true praise requires this. God always expects praise as the first-fruits of any meeting and it should come first to bring down the anointing.

Apart from praise in the services or meetings it has a special place in our individual lives as believers. God has always wanted a special people to praise Him and when the Jews rejected Jesus this privilege passed to the Church. The prophecy about Jesus in Isaiah 61 is that He would give us 'a garment of praise instead of a spirit of despair.' This is meant to shine out in these days of doom and gloom. Christians should never be in despair for Jesus promised that He would never leave us nor forsake us. We need to put on the garment of praise and praise the Lord because Jesus has given us this ministry.

There has been some controversy over whether God expects us to praise Him for everything or not. There is no verse that says that we should. The closest passage is in 1 Thessalonians: 'Be joyful always; pray continually; give thanks in all circumstances, for this is God's will for you in Christ Jesus.' (1 Thessalonians 5:16–18 NIV.)

It really depends on the view you take of the overall plan of God and His sovereignty. In other words if God determines *everything* that happens to you then you praise Him *for* everything. If disaster and tragedy strike you praise God for it and believe He will use it for His glory.

'And we know that in all things God works for the good of those who love him, who have been called according to his purpose.' (Romans 8:28 NIV.)

This assumes that God's will is always done, when actually this is not the case. It is God's will that everyone should be saved, for example, and clearly they are not because of free-will. The same applies to sin. God's will is that we do not sin but clearly we do. It is an overstatement of the truth to praise God *for* everything because it assumes that everything is His responsibility. If a major disaster strikes and the devil manages to ruin a man's life and ministry by deceiving him into sin it would be extraordinary to praise God for it, as it is in effect a victory for the devil's strategy. If sickness and death hits a family it is almost a form of fatalism to praise God for this wonderful 'blessing'. The truth is rather to be found in the passage quoted: *In* everything give thanks. This is much sounder because it implies that despite everything God is God and He is worthy to be praised no matter what happens. He is sovereign and will use past disasters for His glory and turn cursing into blessing. In some cases individuals needed a disaster to turn them to the Lord for salvation. In those cases it is valid to praise God *for* the disaster because it led to salvation. As believers we should praise God for who He is and if we have committed our way to Him praise Him that He is able to keep what is committed to Him (2 Timothy 1:12). We praise Him because our life is in His hands and He will allow certain things to happen to us. It is in these situations that we learn to praise the Lord and acknowledge His sovereignty. There are of course things to thank Him for but we need to discern what is from the hand of the Lord and what is not. Let us consider the example of David.

David got caught in the sins of adultery and murder. As a man who praised the Lord we could reasonably have expected a Psalm praising the Lord for the situation and how God used it if this was the correct principle. In fact Psalm 51 implies that he desired to praise God for Himself:

'O Lord, open my lips,
and my mouth will declare your praise.'
(Psalm 51:15 NIV.)

Nathan told David that because of his sin the child would die (2 Samuel 12:14). David still prayed for seven days and nights but the child died anyway. David did not then praise God for the child's death, but acknowledged that the life belonged to God and He took it.

'Then David got up from the ground. After he had washed, put on lotions and changed his clothes, he went into the house of the Lord and worshipped.' (2 Samuel 12:20 NIV.)

He praised God in the situation which was his own doing, not the Lord's. His servants were surprised and couldn't understand it. However because David honoured God his next son was Solomon and in the lineage of Jesus. The Lord sent a special word to David that He loved Solomon, which must have been a great encouragement to David.

Most of us have had some disaster in the past or may yet face one in the future. Whether we feel we should praise God for everything or in everything the main point is that we should praise Him because He is God. As we acknowledge Him in this way it releases His power into the situation so that we know that His grace is sufficient. This is something we need to learn to do as a habit. It is part of His stated will. We need to rejoice in the Lord and know the joy of the Lord as our strength, to pray about everything as we saw in the previous chapter and to give thanks in all circumstances. Our salvation alone deserves constant praise. May we be numbered among those who will honour the Lord with a sacrifice of praise and go out at the head of the army to praise our way to victory.

13

The Lord is with you, mighty warrior
Judges 6:13

We have seen earlier how faith can be quenched and that without faith it is impossible to please God. We are called to walk by faith and not by sight and to increase our faith from hearing the Word of God. Whatever place of faith you may currently have God wants to move you on from there into ever increasing faith. If you feel you have little or none God still wants you to start using what you have. We can always find reasons why not to move in faith and settle for the blessings we have already and what is easily attainable. If you want to please God it has to be by walking in faith. There is no other way, for whatever is not of faith is sin. *Those who move in faith please God.* At some point we have to move out of the natural and start walking by faith in the Spirit.

The best example of getting started is Gideon, because he was such a weak and feeble character! Very few people are worse than Gideon yet when the angel of the Lord appears he greets him: 'The *Lord* is with you, *mighty warrior*.' (Judges 6:13 NIV.)

Gideon was far from that in the natural as he himself points out – he is from the weakest clan in Manasseh and he is the least in his family. In other words he would not be a natural leader but the lowest of the low, just the kind of material God is after. It's a good starting point because it shows we all qualify to be used. The angel of the Lord speaks *in faith* and sees him as he will be. No matter how you see yourself naturally you need the eyes of faith to see yourself as God sees you, which may be radically different. The fullness of Jesus lives in you and you have the indwelling Holy Spirit, which Gideon did not have, so you have a built in advantage.

Gideon's immediate reaction is to query the statement that God is with him. Instead of receiving it by faith he reacts with his mind.

'"But sir," Gideon replied, "if the *Lord* is with us, why has all this happened to us? Where are all his wonders that our fathers told us about when they said, 'Did not the Lord bring us up out of Egypt?' But now the *Lord* has abandoned us and put us into the hand of Midian."' (Judges 6:13 NIV.)

You may well ask why things have happened to you if you're supposed to be a victorious believer living by the promises of God. Indeed it may even seem as if God has abandoned you, although it's not true. The answer the angel of the Lord gives is: '*Go in the strength you have* and save Israel out of Midian's hand. Am I not sending you?' (Judges 6:14 NIV.)

As far as God is concerned we have the strength *now* and have to make a start moving in what we have by faith. The argument was not over whether he had it or not. It was enough that God was sending him and it should be enough that Jesus is sending us.

The next question is 'How can *I* save Israel? What can *I* do? We all wonder how we are going to achieve what God wants but the answer is clear. God is going to do it: 'The *Lord* answered, "I will be with you, and you will strike down the Midianites as if they were but one man."' (Judges 6:16 NIV.)

Next Gideon wants a sign! Sometimes we are the same.

We want proof that God is in it because we prefer to walk by sight and not faith. The Lord was very gracious to Gideon and gave him a sign as a spur to faith.

'The angel of the Lord said to him, "Take the meat and the unleavened bread, place them on this rock, and pour out the broth." And Gideon did so. With the tip of the staff that was in his hand, the angel of the *Lord* touched the meat and the unleavened bread. Fire flared from the rock, consuming the meat and the bread. And the angel of the *Lord* disappeared. When Gideon realised it was the angel of the *Lord*, he exclaimed, "Ah, Sovereign *Lord!* I have seen the angel of the *Lord* face to face!"' (Judges 6:20–22 NIV.)

Later that night the Lord told him to start moving in faith and cut down his father's Asherah pole and destroy his altar to Baal. He did it by night because he was afraid to do it during the day. At least he did it. It is possible to get so fearful about moving in the Spirit and in faith that you won't move at all. Gideon gets over that first hurdle of obedience and God saw him through. He still nevertheless had unbelief so we have the story of the fleeces not once but twice! This is not a distinguished example of moving by faith and we should not be putting fleeces out to God. They are a sign of unbelief and immaturity and we are not to put God to the test in this way unless he specifically invites us to or allows it, in which case the result will be the opposite of what would naturally happen. It is not meant to be used as part of the process of guidance and it is no credit to Gideon that he did it. Even after his fleeces he is still in fear. God spoke to him the night of the attack:

'"Get up, go down against the camp, because I am going to give it into your hands. If you are afraid to attack, go down to the camp with your servant Purah and listen to what they are saying. Afterwards, you will be encouraged to attack the camp."' (Judges 7:9–11 NIV.)

If he had not been in fear he would not have gone down,

but he does and hears the dream of the barley loaf. Finally the penny drops!

'Gideon arrived just as a man was telling a friend his dream. "I had a dream," he was saying. "A round loaf of barley bread came tumbling into the Midianite camp. It struck the tent with such force that the tent overturned and collapsed." His friend responded, "This can be nothing other than the sword of Gideon son of Joash, the Israelite. God has given the Midianites and the whole camp into his hands."

When Gideon heard the dream and its interpretation, he worshipped God. He returned to the camp of Israel and called out, "Get up! The *Lord* has given the Midianite camp into your hands."' (Judges 7:13–15 NIV.)

Interestingly after the victory the Israelites wanted him to be their king. Gideon now in faith gives the right answer as we saw in chapter one.

'But Gideon told them, "I will not rule over you, nor will my son rule over you. *The Lord will rule over you*."' (Judges 8:23 NIV.)

He did however lapse into sin and make an ephod which became a snare to him and his family.

The story of Gideon illustrates how hard it can be for God to get us moving in faith. We make excuses and prefer God to choose someone else. When faced with a sick person we can reach out in faith and pray or leave them to use their own faith and hope someone else will pray for them. When we encounter oppression we may prefer not to deal with it rather than confront it in the name of Jesus. If we lack provision we may look to the State and not the Lord. We need to ask God to make us men of faith who truly will please Him.

Consider all the promises of God which are the basis of walking in faith. Either God is a liar or they are true. There is no middle position. They are all true in the realm of faith.

That means that if you believe and apply any promise by faith you will find it to be true in your own experience. They are like the Promised Land but have to be possessed and the obstacles and giants have to be overcome.

When the spies came back from the land they had seen the fruit but also the problems. The result was that they decided it was too hard because there was considerable opposition. God had promised them the land and Caleb chose to believe what God said and he was in faith about moving in. God's judgement on the unbelieving spies was forty years in the wilderness. You either move into the promises by faith or you are stuck in the wilderness. God's word to the people is: 'not one of them will ever see the land I promised on oath to their forefathers. No-one who has treated me with contempt will ever see it. But because my servant Caleb has a different spirit and follows me wholeheartedly, I will bring him to the land he went to, and his descendants will inherit it.' (Numbers 14:23–24 NIV.)

We have to be of that different spirit and not see the obstacles. God wants us to move in faith and to be whole-hearted about it. It is the only way to please Him. You start simply by believing all the promises of God and applying them. As you prove them to be true God moves you on in faith and into situations where you have to reach out for more. We need to go in the strength we already have from the Holy Spirit. It is a matter of choice to do so. Jesus was grieved at the unbelief of His day and frequently called the people 'O ye of little faith' or 'O faithless generation.' This should never be true of the Body of Christ with all that God has invested in us. Jesus asks the question 'When the Son of Man comes will he find faith on the earth?' (Luke 18:8 NIV). It is a real question. In these days of science and reason that seek to rationalise away the Lord, God wants a visible people walking by faith on the earth. The question is whether we are willing to please God and be one of those people. The answer is up to you.

14

I chose you that you go and bear fruit
John 15:16

At the very beginning of creation we read of God's first recorded words to Adam: 'Be fruitful and multiply in number; fill the earth and subdue it' (Genesis 1:28 NIV). The command is to be fruitful, which is part of God's purpose for Man. This is quite separate from multiplying, which relates to filling the earth and refers to subduing the earth so that it is productive and brings forth fruit. This is an important principle to see because God wanted Adam to exercise rulership as part of his fruitfulness. In other words he would be directly involved in producing order and being in authority over the animal and plant kingdoms. He was to be in control and as long as he was in fellowship with God abundance, prosperity and fruitfulness would result. The same principle applies to redeemed Man in the walk of the Spirit. We are to be fruitful. When Jesus spoke to the disciples he told them: 'You did not choose me, but I chose yo to *go and bear fruit* – fruit that will last.' (John 15:16 NIV.)

The fruit we are to bear is the type that will last and determine our reward in heaven, which is of course eternal and will last forever. In this chapter we shall look at the fruit that the Holy Spirit wants to bring forth in our lives and how to achieve abundant fruitfulness.

All fruit starts as a seed and when we are saved there is a seed planted within us. It comes from the Holy Spirit tree and is the very nature of Jesus, who was filled with the Spirit and fruitful. There is no fruit apart from Jesus (John 15:5) and the Holy Spirit will produce the nature of Jesus in us to the degree that we co-operate.

The parable of the sower indicates what can happen to the source of the fruit, namely the seed. Without restating the parable in full the seed is the Word of God and some fell on the path, some on rocky ground, some among thorns and some on good ground. Jesus gives the explanation:

'"Listen to what the parable of the sower means: When anyone hears the message about the kingdom and does not understand it, the evil one comes and snatches away what was sown in his heart. This is the seed sown along the path. What was sown on rocky places is the man who hears the word and at once receives it with joy. But since he has no root, he lasts only a short time. When trouble or persecution comes because of the word, he quickly falls away. What was sown among the thorns is the man who hears the word, but worries of this life and the deceitfulness of wealth choke it, making it unfruitful. But what was sown on good soil is the man who hears the word and understands it. He produces a crop, yielding a hundred, sixty or thirty times what was sown."' (Matthew 13:18–23 NIV.)

The seed is supposed to produce fruit in each one of us but we determine how great that fruit shall be. This is true both of salvation and of the seed of the fruit of the Spirit. Galatians 5 is in essence a contrast between the walk of the Spirit and the walk of the flesh. There is a choice hence the exhortation 'So I say, live by the Spirit'. We shall now consider the parable of the sower in relation to the seed of the fruit of the Spirit, for the principle is identical. The first seed falls by the wayside. Jesus relates it to the message of the kingdom that is neither received nor understood and the devil therefore snatches it away. This can happen to the seed of the fruit of the Spirit for if it is neither received nor understood it will not be watered and the devil will snatch away the idea that we should be fruitful at all. This happens when only salvation is preached and nothing more. It is assumed that any fruit will be self-germinating and automatic. Part of that message is that the gifts are not for now either! We need to be sure that the concept of fruitfulness is not snatched away by the father of lies and the accuser of the brethren.

The rocky ground is the man who initially desires to be fruitful for God but has no root to reach down to the nourishment. He does not read the Word because there is something good on TV, he doesn't go to the prayer meeting because it means getting up early after the late night movie and definitely doesn't fast because he'd feel hungry! This kind of shallowness will not produce fruit because of all the rocks in the ground. There's an initial enthusiasm after salvation but the spiritual life then gets too hard because some effort is required!

The thorns and thistles are more common than generally realised. We tend to assume that we are of course the good ground and can deceive ourselves that we are better than is the case.

'Do not merely listen to the word, and so deceive yourselves. *Do what it says.*' (James 1:22 NIV.)

Unless we are actively putting into practice the principles of the Word of God we will be deceived into thinking that we are following the Lord when we are merely onlookers.

Two of the main thorns are the worries of this life and the deceitfulness of wealth. These prevent the fruit of the Spirit from growing to full maturity. If we can weed out the thorns and thistles then we shall have abundant fruit.

The fruit all comes from the same seed. You do not produce some of the fruit and not others.

The fruit of the Spirit is in essence a description of the character of Jesus. We are to be like Him, and aware of those things that hinder this. 'Therefore, since we are surrounded by such a great cloud of witnesses, let us throw off everything that hinders and the sin that so easily entangles, and let us run with perseverance the race marked out for us. Let us fix our eyes on Jesus, the author and perfector of our faith, who for the joy set before him endured the cross, scorning its shame, and sat down at the right hand of the throne of God.' (Hebrews 12:1–2 NIV.)

In the context of a race any excess weight slows you down and you miss your potential. With the gardening picture the problem is both the soil and the weeds. God nevertheless is keeping an eye on us as His sons and will correct and discipline us.

'God disciplines us for our good, that we may share in his holiness. No discipline seems pleasant at the time, but painful. Later on, however, it produces a harvest of righteousness and peace for those who have been trained by it.

Therefore, strengthen your feeble arms and weak knees! Make level paths for your feet, so that the lame may not be disabled, but rather healed.' (Hebrews 12:10–13 NIV.)

The fruit of the Spirit and the harvest of righteousness and peace are in essence the same thing, therefore we need to see discipline in a positive way and not despise God's ways of making us fruitful. We reap what we sow and if we sow to the Spirit we shall reap a bountiful harvest in the form of a really fruitful life for God.

The devil is also sowing as the parable of the wheat and tares illustrates but we sow too. The seventh of the things the Lord hates is a man who sows discord among brothers (Proverbs 6:19). Control of the tongue is the supreme objective of self-control and God wants the Holy Spirit to control our tongues. One of the reasons that tongues were given to the Church at Pentecost is because God wanted His people to praise Him with a pure tongue and that had to come from the Holy Spirit. This is still true in the natural area and God wants your uncontrollable tongue (James 3:8)! It is He who will produce the fruit of self-control as we yield to the Spirit of God. The fruit of the Spirit is the corporate result of the process of turning seed into ripe fruit. You don't have some but not others, for example patience but not self-control! They are all part of that same fruit. It starts off as a seed but it's all there in potential. First you see the blossom immediately after salvation, then it falls off sometimes to the surprise of the person who expected it to be that way permanently. After blossom you have a tiny little piece of fruit that forms. If you pick it and eat it you will find that it is hard, green and bitter and you would reject it, but it is still nevertheless fruit. Only in the later stages does the fruit come into ripeness and is visibly identifiable as fruit because the colour changes. Too often we only think of fruit as fully formed and ripe and fail to recognise the stages of growth. Growth takes time and we are being ripened by God into mature fruit. It need not take so very long and will be affected by the climate we are in. If you are in a greenhouse where there is warmth and water you will grow that more rapidly. Equally true is the reverse, namely that if you are stuck out in the icy cold and not fed or watered the fruit will be less and take much longer to produce. Fruit is important because it shows what kind of tree you are from and even if you are producing fruit God will still prune you and you will be cut back regularly to produce even more fruit. It is the result of a Spirit led life and does glorify God as Jesus says: 'This is to my father's glory that *you bear much fruit*, showing yourselves to be my disciples.' (John 15:8 NIV.)

This is why we are told to recognise people by their fruit because it shows what kind of seed is inside them.

In the parable of the sower Jesus said that the seed would bear fruit, some thirtyfold, some sixtyfold and some one hundredfold. There are two different views of the meaning of this. Some consider that the seed has equal potential in each person and that we can all produce one hundredfold as our maximum potential because the seed of the Holy Spirit is capable of this. If you then produce sixtyfold you have achieved sixty per cent of your potential and similarly thirtyfold is thirty per cent. In other words it all depends on the soil and how we feed and water that seed.

The other view is that believers have different potential by the sovereign grace of God. Some are capable of much, others of less and God is looking for faithfulness. This view is supported by the parable of the talents where they were given different amounts. If you are a thirtyfolder in potential and produce thirtyfold then you have done equally as well as the potential hundredfolder who produces a hundredfold. Actually if you produce thirty and he produces ninety you have done better as far as God is concerned even if an outside observer thinks the ninetyfolder has been three times as productive as you!

Whichever interpretation you choose the key is to achieve your maximum potential and not be concerned if others appear to be doing better. There is tremendous potential in the Holy Spirit to be really productive for the kingdom and it is also true that we can quench the Spirit and limit the fruitfulness. It is up to us to keep our soil weed free and open to the light of the Word of God and the living water that comes from Jesus. There is a day coming when God who is no man's debtor will reward those who have faithfully served Him and led a fruitful life. It is indeed a high calling. There is no easy way or soft option for the man of God. We have to take up our cross daily, die to self and follow Jesus.

Perhaps the best way to conclude is to consider what Paul wrote to Timothy and pray that God will be pleased with us on that day when we finally meet the One we seek to serve: 'I have fought the good fight, I have finished the race, I have kept the faith. Now there is in store for me the crown of righteousness, which the Lord, the righteous Judge, will award to me on that day – and not only to me, but also to *all* who have longed for his appearing.' (2 Timothy 4:7–8 NIV.)

When we meet Jesus may He be able to say 'Well done, good and faithful servant. Enter into the joy of your master' (Matthew 25:21).

Many people towards the end of their natural life regret the missed opportunities and the wasted years, when they chose to live for themselves rather than God. Solomon started off walking with the Lord but the cares of this life and the deceitfulness of riches led him astray. When he looked back and wrote the Book of Ecclesiastes he wished he had been wholehearted towards God. He discovered that the fear of the Lord is the beginning of wisdom and that the commandments of the Lord are the route to happiness and he wished he had followed them. May we make the most of the days God has given us and determine afresh that we will be led by the Spirit of God, living a fruitful life worthy of our high calling.

'Now all has been heard;
here is the conclusion of the matter:
Fear God and keep his commandments,
for this is the whole duty of man.'
(Ecclesiastes 12:13–14 NIV.)

15

They were all together in one place

Acts 2:1

Not only do we have the Holy Spirit indwelling every single believer, but He also dwells in us corporately as the Body of Christ. We are described as living stones being built into a building, with Jesus Himself as the cornerstone.

'As you come to him, the living Stone – rejected by men but chosen by God and precious to him – you also, like living stones, are being built into a spiritual house to be a holy priesthood, offering spiritual sacrifices acceptable to God through Jesus Christ.' (1 Peter 2:4–5 NIV.)

As Christians we no longer have the option or luxury of an individualistic life because we are part of something bigger than a group of individuals with the Lord in common. We therefore need to see ourselves not as 'going to church' or the meeting, but being the Church and functioning with the other members in a unified way. As part of the Body of Christ each part is necessary and matters, whether the individual believes that to be the case or not (1 Corinthians 12:14–26). If one part suffers then every part suffers. If we are not feeling the suffering of those members of the Body who hurt, including those in prison around the world, then we are not functioning fully as the Body of Christ. Our lives are meant to be interdependent in such a way that we can meaningfully bear one another's burdens and so fulfil the law of Christ to love one another (Galatians 6:2). There is still in most of us too much of self, too much individualism, which is more cultural than biblical and part of the spirit of the age. It's also part of the old sin nature that needs to be put to death.

'Each of you should look not only to your own interests, but also to the interests of others. Your attitude should be the same as that of Christ Jesus:' (Philippians 2:4–5 NIV).

Even in the Body of Christ there are ministers who belong nowhere and are accountable to nobody. God wants His children to be part of His family in more than theory and to have a meaningful relationship with each other. The world is supposed to say 'See how they love one another'. In fact you hear more often 'Why can't they agree?' Renewal clearly has to touch us in this area much more than has happened hitherto.

This final chapter considers the marks of the New Testament church, all of which can be quite easily restored if we want them enough. The passage from which they are taken is Acts 2.

'They *devoted themselves* to the apostles' *teaching* and to the *fellowship*, to the *breaking of bread* and to *prayer*. Everyone was filled with awe, and many wonders and miraculous signs were done by the apostles. All the believers were *together* and had everything in common. Selling their possessions and goods, they *gave* to anyone as he had need. Every day they continued to *meet together* in the temple courts. They broke bread in their homes and *ate together* with glad and sincere hearts, *praising God* and enjoying the favour of the people. And the Lord added to their number daily those who were being saved.' (Acts 2:42–47 NIV.)

First of all they were devoted and committed to a programme of teaching to bring them to maturity. This was far more than even regular Sunday teaching or cassettes.

The commitment was such that like the pearl of great price everything else was jettisoned in order to devote their whole energy to this objective. In some cases this included jobs, for the teaching went on every day and if you were tied up you missed it. Often it would go right on into the late hours (Acts 20:7–11). This is not to suggest that believers hand in their notice but rather to consider our work in the tent-making context as Paul did, where he worked to support his ministry which was his main goal, and was willing to do a humble job that fitted in with his travels and ministry. In those days teaching had to be verbal because some could not read and books were not available anyway, so the way they showed their devotion was by attending a continual programme of spoken teaching. In today's context it means devotion to Bible study and reading. New Christians generally have an insatiable appetite to read but many lose it. Consider what would happen to a church or fellowship where everyone spent just a couple of hours every day doing this, rather than expecting always to be spoon-fed. The objective is multiplication and fruitfulness so that today's learners are tomorrow's teachers. There should be a programme of recommended reading of the Bible or teaching cassettes so that the initial enthusiasm and devotion can be encouraged and directed. The basics need to be systematically covered. Unfortunately they are not covered in the majority of books on basic teaching, primarily because the emphasis has moved away from teaching on, for example, water baptism or the baptism in the Spirit, which are really basics. To study these you may have to use a topical Bible, concordance, or read a single book on each subject. The basics are listed in Hebrews 6.

'Therefore let us leave the elementary teachings about Christ and go on to maturity, not laying again the foundation of *repentance* from acts that lead to death, and of *faith* in God, instruction about *baptism*s, the *laying on of* *hands*, the *resurrection* of the dead, and *eternal judgement*.' (Hebrews 6:1–3 NIV.)

These were the basic areas where the believers received instruction as part of their grounding in the faith. In my own experience I was taught none of these as a young believer, and have never yet heard teaching on the laying on of hands. We have a lot of catching up to do if we want to be like the early Church. We all have access to the Bible so that we can learn about them ourselves and ask the Holy Spirit to give us revelation. The Body of Christ needs the teaching ministries to nourish and build up the Church, and for a fresh devotion to hearing and applying the pure Word of God.

They devoted themselves to the fellowship. The mutual commitment of a group of believers to each other cannot happen if you rarely meet and split your life between work, home and church. There is a great need for love and belonging together in the Body of Christ, because many find refuge there from a harsh world. We need to establish that sense of togetherness, that we have thrown in our lot with the other believers, whoever they are, because they too are the Lord's. Devotion to the fellowship is like the triangle with Jesus at the top, you at the base in one corner and other believers in the other corner. As you and the other believers move closer to the Lord you move closer to one another. Equally as you move closer to one another you move closer to the Lord. We really do need each other and to know that the commitment is mutual – us to the fellowship and the fellowship to us. Those who have lived abroad will have had some experience of this in the natural area. The British stick together with others from the old country and have a form of comradeship simply because they are British! God wants far more than that because we are His. Where you have this really functioning the believers hate being away, even on holiday, and long to get

146

back. It is very important that believers find where they belong in the Body of Christ and are committed to that group of believers so that the others can also be committed to them. This is more than membership and cannot be forced. It has to come from a real sense of belonging.

The breaking of bread to which they devoted themselves was the 'agape' love feast, as it was known until the second century when it effectively stopped due to religious leaders turning it into a service and away from its proper purpose. It was not communion as such, but it was more than an ordinary meal. The 'breaking of bread' or 'communion' which we now have is very different from the practice of the early Church. Because we have kept the name we tend to assume that they did what we do, but that is not the case. Basically it was a fellowship meal together that would have led on into choruses, praise and worship and really bonded together the believers. Just as Jesus was made known in the breaking of bread at Emmaus (Luke 24:30), so He presences Himself with those who meet for a meal in this way. They basically came together to eat (1 Corinthians 11:33) and after eating a meal would remember Jesus in the passing of the bread and wine before going on into the meeting, almost like a thank you after the meal. The apostles may well have based it on the practice of Jesus. It was after supper that He passed the cup (1 Corinthians 11:25) and they then sang a hymn (Mark 14:26). This was probably a regular feature of the disciples fellowship together, although this is the only reference. Jesus did much of His ministry in the context of a meal, and was criticised for eating with publicans and sinners in this way. Meals are a good opportunity for fellowship and when Jesus met Zacchaeus, for example, He invited Himself to Zacchaeus' home to fellowship over a meal. This ministry is sometimes neglected and is included within the whole area of hospitality. It must be based on the Luke 14 principle of need, rather than inviting those you like. We should in fact be doing both without partiality, but particularly to the needy in the Body, the lonely, the widows, the single parent families and those who may look fine but are not.

'Then Jesus said to his host, "When you give a luncheon or dinner, do not invite your friends, your brothers or relatives, or your rich neighbours; if you do, they may invite you back and so you will be repaid. But when you give a banquet, invite the poor, the crippled, the lame, the blind, and you will be blessed. Although they cannot repay you, you will be repaid at the resurrection of the righteous."' (Luke 14:12–14 NIV.)

No-one in the New Testament Church would have slipped through the pastoral net and been excluded, because the devotion to one another was so deep. It is important to differentiate between the breaking of bread and communion or the Lord's supper because of the underlying assumption that they are the same. The Lord's supper in fact replaced the Passover for the believers as Jesus was the Passover Lamb (1 Corinthians 5:7) and the early Church recognised this. The breaking of bread was the regular fellowshipping over a meal and was the normal practice for the first two hundred years of the Church. In seeking to return to early church life we need more fellowship over meals rather than more communion services, which in their current liturgical form tend to be an individual communion with God through the priest rather than a corporate communion with one another.

They were devoted to prayer. If Christians were even half as devoted our lives individually and corporately would be transformed. Consider what proportion of your church or fellowship regularly attend a prayer meeting, for it is there that the devotion can be seen. Because we are all responsible for our own time it is nobody else's fault. There is nothing to stop us being devoted and going, whatever anybody else does or does not do, but if there is little prayer there will be little power and little effectiveness. Devotion to prayer brings down the power of God.

'After they prayed, the place where they were meeting was shaken. And they were all filled with the Holy Spirit and spoke the word of God boldly.' (Acts 4:31 NIV.)

Only the 120 devoted to prayer were in the Upper Room when the power of the Holy Spirit fell on them. These were the prayers and they in all probability represented less than twenty per cent of the initial Church. Initially they were a group of around thirty as they returned to Jerusalem from the ascension on the Mount of Olives (Acts 1:13–14). The number depends on how many women were there at that time. The early core of believers was 120 (Acts 1:15) and this 120 was present on the day of Pentecost (Acts 2:1). The question is where were the others to whom Jesus had appeared, as he appeared to over 500 at one time (1 Corinthians 15:6). Paul describes them as 'over five hundred of the brothers' so they were believers but somehow had not joined with the early Church, or if they had were not there with them praying on the day of Pentecost. The 120 were devoted prayers. 'They all joined together constantly in prayer, along with the women and Mary the mother of Jesus, and his brothers' (Acts 1:14 NIV).

The real point is that those devoted to being together to pray received the power and even if we are one of the 500 who have had a revelation of Jesus there is a better place still, namely being locked together with other believers seeking God in prayer. Maybe some of the 500 heard about Pentecost and kicked themselves for not being there, determining never to miss another prayer meeting! Things happen at prayer meetings where there is a devotion to seeking the Lord and prayer needs to be a very high priority, not just alone at home, but with the other members of the Body of Christ. Ideally they would all pray together as a Body, but if this is impossible then at least in areas. If we want early church power we need early church prayer.

Many signs and wonders were done. There has to be a link between the teaching, fellowship, breaking of bread, prayer and signs following. Where the Body is together and functioning biblically the Lord blesses (Psalm 133). Perhaps the current absence of the visible power of God in some places has to do with the absence of these other factors as well. Certainly where they are being restored the signs are beginning to follow. If we were less concerned with the signs and more with the glory of God and representing Jesus on the earth they would just naturally flow from manifesting the life of Jesus within us.

They were together and had all things in common. This is often misunderstood, because if they had all sold their houses there would have been an immediate housing crisis to deal with! In fact they all re-evaluated all their possessions, sold what was not needed and used the money to meet the needs of those who had nothing. They had probably been forced to leave home through being Christians, and may well have joined the Church with literally nothing but the clothes they stood in. Faced with a situation like that a holiday home at Tiberias or Eilat looked quite ridiculous so those who had houses sold the second one. We know that they kept some to fellowship in, because they broke bread from house to house (Acts 2:46). The key lies in the willingness to give everything to the Lord.

'All the believers were one in heart and mind. No-one claimed that any of his possessions was his own, but they *shared everything* they had. With great power the apostles continued to testify to the resurrection of the Lord Jesus, and much grace was with them all. There were no needy persons among them. From time to time those who owned lands or houses sold them, brought the money from the sales and put it at the apostles' feet, and it was distributed to any-one as he had need.' (Acts 4:32–35 NIV.)

It is quite possible for the Body of Christ to return to a greater degree of sharing, and not considering possessions to be for our own exclusive use. The early Church had a real revelation that they had been bought by the Lord along with everything they had, and it was all available for the Body. It was seen as God's and not their own. The spirit of the world has infiltrated the Church if we think that all we have is ours for our own exclusive enjoyment. We can return to the concept of sharing if we are closely knitted together as a fellowship. This does not necessarily mean all putting your income into one pool and everyone drawing out what they need, although some have found this to work. Rather it is an openness to acknowledge that everything comes from God, that we have personal stewardship and accountability, and to be willing to be led by the Holy Spirit in giving to the needs of the Body. Giving should be done with maximum free-will, in secret and in faith, not under compulsion, publicly and as a sort of levy where faith is not exercised (2 Corinthians 9:7). Giving is in essence sowing in the kingdom and an investment in the future. We will reap what we sow.

God added to their number. Where there is life and commitment in the fellowship growth will occur. This is the best form of evangelism, not just preaching the gospel but living it. Where love and power are evident those who seek after truth will find the Lord. We should be proud to bring visitors to our meetings, because of what the Lord has done among us. If life is there unbelievers will discern it. Paul expects unbelievers to be at the services (1 Corinthians 14:22–25), and for them to fall down and worship God, exclaiming, 'God is really among you!' if the Body functions with tongues and prophecy. That is a further reason for having meetings of this kind, because they have an evangelistic role as well and can bring in far more numerical growth than the conventional type of mission. It also makes follow-up that much easier.

The early Church was not without its problems, primarily to do with the change from Judaism and the synagogue system to the New Covenant with its new structure, authority and type of worship. Because we have in many cases churches that are on the Judaistic model of priest and people, it will be quite a radical step to return to the New Testament model. It is nevertheless possible if you want it badly enough. As mentioned earlier you do need a good measure of local autonomy and to use what freedom you have to implement some of the principles. If we are willing to live as the early Church did, be as devoted as they were and walk in faith and power as they did, then we will see God working mightily among us as they did. Jesus is the same, yesterday, today and forever, and the promise of the Spirit is for *us*.

'And you will receive the gift of the Holy Spirit. The promise is for you and your children and *all who are far off* – *for all* whom the Lord our God will call.'

With many other words he warned them; and he pleaded with them, 'Save yourselves from this corrupt generation.' (Acts 2:38–40 NIV.)

If we do not have the power it is not because the promise is invalid and applies to a different dispensation. It is because God gives the Holy Spirit to those who obey Him (Acts 5:32) and if we reject biblical truth the Holy Spirit is grieved and restricted in His work. In these last days before Jesus returns we have a wonderful opportunity to see the power of the Holy Spirit at work in our nation, if we will do His work His way.

Before concluding this chapter and the book we need to

consider where we are in God's timetable. There really is not much time left to us. Many have said this before, of course, with the result that it seems as if we are crying 'wolf', but it is doubtful whether we even have forty years left. Certain specific prophecies still have to be fulfilled before the Lord returns but they could all happen very quickly. Just forty years ago there had been no nuclear bomb on Japan, we were at war with Germany and Russia was our ally. Men had not been to the moon and international jet travel was in its infancy. Israel was not even a nation. God has forbidden us the knowledge of the hour of the Lord's return, but Jesus does want us to know the *season*. '"Now learn this lesson from the fig-tree: As soon as its twigs get tender and its leaves come out, you know that summer is near. Even so, when you see all these things, you know that it is near, right at the door. I tell you the truth, this generation will certainly not pass away until all these things have happened. Heaven and earth will pass away, but my words will never pass away."' (Matthew 24:32–35 NIV.)

Jesus is referring to the whole scenario of the last days and gives us some detailed knowledge of what to expect. The fig tree refers prophetically to Israel, which became a nation in 1948. That may not initially seem obvious, but if there was a prophecy about a shamrock or a maple leaf it would be as obvious to us now that it meant Ireland and Canada as the fig tree did to them at that time. Eschatologists differ on the interpretation of 'this generation'. Some believe it means 'this race', in other words it was a promise that the Jews would always exist as a race, with or without a homeland. Others believe that it refers to a Jewish generation of forty years and that Jesus will return in 1988, i.e. the key year forty years or one generation after the establishment of the State of Israel. Another view is that the generation born in 1948 will be the last one, i.e. if you add three score and ten years to 1948 you come up with 2018. We do not know the precise time, but whatever it is time is very short within which to bring in the harvest of believers. God needs His people to be prepared and ready to work for Him now. There is an urgency about the work of God, and all of us have an involvement and a responsibility. We need to dedicate what remaining years we may have to serving the Lord with all we've got. The end will not build up to a predictable crescendo. It will be like the days of Noah and life will seem to go on as if it will never end (Matthew 24:38–39). Jesus tells us to watch and be ready for He will come like a thief in the night. It will then be too late for regrets. In conclusion consider the words of Jesus in Revelation 22:20–21, 'He who testifies to these things says, "Yes, I am coming soon." Amen. Come, Lord Jesus.

The grace of the Lord Jesus be with God's people. Amen.'

GOOD HEALTH!

Should a Christian put his trust in God or in medicine? Can a Christian take no heed for his health and then ask God to bail him out when he becomes ill.

Trevor Martin looks first at the theory, then the practice of good health. In the first part of the book he examines the relationship between medical science and supernatural healing, questioning the modern assumption that medicine is authoritative and 'right'. In the second part he sets everyday living within this context. Our bodies are God's gift, wonderfully made; yet how poorly we care for the temple of God's Spirit. Trevor Martin demonstrates how good health affects our relationships, enjoyment of leisure, coping effectively with stress and living life to the praise of God.

GOD CAN DO IT FOR YOU

Do you doubt the existence of God?
Are you in physical pain?
Do you feel at the end of your endurance?
Do you suffer from a disease or handicap?

Ian Andrews has a clear call and an anointed ministry. He is a man through whom the Holy Spirit can flow in message, wisdom and power to bring healing to God's people and, sometimes, in the mercy of God, to those who have no interest in or expectation of a relationship with God.

It is our prayer that those who read may step out in faith to receive God's love-gift for them.

LETTERS FOR AUNTY FLO

A light hearted approach to the serious subject of Radical Discipleship, with a set of discussion starters for groups.

- David wanted to buy an expensive car, God made him buy a banger.
- David thought peace meant no war, God told him about shalom.
- David thought only other people were racist, God made him think again.
- David went along with the crowd, God helped him go anti-flow

Graham Young is Regional Youth Officer for the Methodist Church in the North of England. He has worked with Christian Aid and the Shaftesbury Project, and is also involved with Traidcraft and the Frontier Youth Trust.

SHARING YOUR FAITH

'I'm too reserved for witnessing'
'My life is witnessing for Christ; that's enough'

Are you one of the casualties who have set out to share your faith and failed? Witnessing is, in the best sense of the word, **easy**. Canned presentations or forced attitudes are not necessary. Selwyn Hughes shows that when you are able to **be yourself** rather than trying to be what you are not, then sharing your faith becomes a delight, not a duty. The only really effective witnessing is natural – witnessing consistent with who and what you are.

This book is a must for all those who want to get out from under the 'guilt trap' brought on by failure in sharing their faith. Selwyn Hughes regards it as his most important book to date.